THE TRUTH OF VALUE

THE TRUTH OF VALUE:

A Defense of Moral and Literary Judgment

Paul Ramsey

Humanities Press
Atlantic Highlands, N.J. 07716

First published in 1985 in the United States of America by Humanities
Press Inc., Atlantic Highlands, NJ 07716

© Copyright 1985 by Humanities Press Inc.

Library of Congress Cataloging in Publication Data

Ramsey, Paul.
The truth of value.

Includes bibliographical references.
1. Christian ethics. 2. Values. 3. Judgment (Ethics) I. Title.
BJ1251.R29 1984   121   83-26603
ISBN 0-391-03058-2

MANUFACTURED IN THE UNITED STATES OF AMERICA

This book is for Earl Miner,

who values truth

Contents

Acknowledgments

Some passages in Chapters 3, 4, 5, and 7 were earlier published, in somewhat different form, in essays in volume 5 (*Literary Criticism and Sociology*) and volume 6 (*The Personality of the Critic*) of the *Yearbook of Comparative Criticism*. Both volumes were edited by Joseph R. Strelka and published by Pennsylvania State University Press in 1973. Permission to reprint has been granted.

Kathyrn L. Horner typed more than one version of the manuscript, with skill and good cheer. Carolyn P. Adcock and Nadine K. Palmer helped with the Bibliography and Index. Edward E. Cahill, Head of the Department of Sociology and Anthropology at the University of Tennessee at Chattanooga, made some thoughtful comments and suggestions.

The directors and staffs of libraries of the University of Tennessee at Chattanooga, Cornell University, Yale University, and the National Library of Scotland have offered me much help and many courtesies.

The University of Chattanooga Foundation supported a research leave offered me by the University of Tennessee at Chattanooga, which I spent as Research Fellow at the Divinity School of Yale University and Associate Fellow of Trumbull College of Yale University, during which time much of the work for, and most of the writing of, the book was done. Paul L. Holmer and others there showed me many kindnesses.

To all involved, my gratitude is hereby expressed.

1

Is That a Fact?: Fact and Monism

The word *fact* is deeply ingrained in our ways of saying, a word quick to the tongue, a word intertwined with concepts deeply entangled in ways of seeing and mis-seeing the world. What is fact? How does it fit, support, exclude? How does it mean? Does it mean?

What is the place of value in a world of fact(s)?[1] That's simple enough to answer. If the world consists of facts and facts alone, and if value is excluded from fact, as the question implies or strongly suggests, then value has no place in reality. Value does not exist. But that's not a scientific or philosophical or any sort of real answer; it's just what the question says. The question begs the question.

Only the question cannot really be even asked. It is inconsistent. For if anyone believes in value, and the world is wholly fact, excluding value, then the world is not wholly fact, since the world consists of all the facts plus the illusion that facts are not all. But if one such illusion exists, then facts are not all. A world that consists of all the facts *plus* one illusion has a very great gulf fixed between it and a world that is merely fact.[2]

What is fact?

A fact is emphatically truth. The emphasis should be on "emphatically." A fact is whatever anyone strongly emphasizes to be truth. A fact is a belief about truth plus a supercharge of emotive confidence.

"A fact is a judgment," said Elroy Bundy.[3]

A fact is a thump on the table. 'That's a *fact*, not any of your fuzzy poetical mooning!'.

Fact is a concept dearly loved, denying the reality and value of love, and thus, that far, a lie.

Fact is — perplexing, when carefully thought on.

1

Fact, says the paranoid, is a conspiracy. A conspiracy of two centuries' duration, strongly bent to separate the good from the known.

Facts are stubborn.

Facts are stubbornly unclear.

Facts are a comfort.

'Everybody knows what *fact* means! It's perverse to deny it.' For instance, in the following:

"The man who classifies facts of any kind whatever, who sees their mutual relation and describes their sequences . . . is a man of science."[4]

That is, facts are just there, separately, prior to relation and sequence but in relation and sequence, describable, clearly distinguished from theory.

"The established fact of evolution."[5]

"The theory of evolution."[6]

That is, theory is fact.

"The facts of mental development . . . are included in the general doctrine of evolution."[7]

Oh, no, theory isn't fact, but very complex facts are contained in doctrines (theories).

"These facts and interpretations of organic evolution."[8]

Well, on the fourth hand . . .

"All of the arguments that the pro-slavery group was able to muster broke against the stubborn fact, which Lincoln persistently thrust in their way, that the Negro was somehow and in some degree a man."[9]

That's a very stubborn truth, like many moral truths, but it works in a very different-sounding kettle of fact from some of the other 'facts', yes?

"If you raise the question" whether the theory fits the facts' . . . you are really only asking whether a description fits another description."[10]

Since fact-description, value-evaluation are the typically linked concepts, that judgment should not sound surprising. But it does. It makes for discomfort, as though it denied that facts were simpler, more basic, more pellucidly and comfortingly there than any description, which is by nature a complex.

People feel comfortable with facts, somehow, as though they know what to do with facts. And yet and yet books discuss and discuss complex philosophical questions of what and where and how facts are.[11] Maybe that proves that philosophy does know what to do with facts; it talks and argues about them, their shiftingness, their unclarity — shiftingly, unclearly.

"Facts are what statements (when true) state; they are not what statements are about."[12]

"The facts speak for themselves."

"The world is the totality of facts."[13]

"Logic deals with every possibility and all possibilities are its facts."[14]

"We can imagine a language in which the proposition 'Archimedes perished at the capture of Syracuse' would be expressed thus: ' the violent death of Archimedes at the capture of Syracuse is fact . . . . *Such a language would have only a single predicate for all judgments, namely, 'is a fact'.*"[15]

One hears from time to time the phrase "moral facts."[16] The words bump more than nuzzle. For in one strong, surging drive of the word *fact*, there cannot be moral facts, since one meaning of *fact*, seldom far below the surface, excludes value.

"False facts are highly injurious to the progress of science."[17]

"The patterns of interpretation they [social philosophies] are constructing reflect such diverse building blocks as facts, pseudofacts, values, and interests."[18]

How do we tell a fact from a pseudofact? Factually? Pseudo-factually?

"What they [the positivists] failed to see was that 'fact' is a term belonging to the vocabulary of historical thought. *Properly* speaking a 'fact' is a thing of the kind which it is the 'business' of historians to ascertain."[19]

The examples so far involve at least the following meanings of *fact*:

Facts are prior to theory. Theory is fact. Facts are truths with immediate moral implications. Facts are any truth whatever. Facts are mere descriptions. Moral truths are facts. All possibilities are fact. Only historical facts are properly facts. Facts are plainly true. Facts can be false. Facts need no interpretations. Facts are in the world. Facts are not in the world. Facts are the world.

People disagree. That's well known and not the point. A point is that people disagree very widely and unconsciously on the use of the word *fact*, a word which is widely felt to be somehow exceptionally and comfortingly clear in its meaning and use.[20] Another point is that meanings of *fact* have two tendencies: to mean any actuality, reality, or truth whatever, *or* to mean matter-of-fact — practical, scientific, value-defused, 'empirical' (whatever that slippery and non-exalting term means). The word comes often trailing its dusty clouds of non-glory and dis-beauty. And when the two tendencies conflate or confound, some very serious and improper question begging can and often does happen.

"To understand them [moral statements], . . . the philosopher asks . . . 'What facts do they state?'"[21] The writer goes on to conclude that moral statements are not statements of truth. Again, not surprising. The push of the language is toward that view. The question begs itself. 'Have you stopped beating your wife?' 'No, sir, I've been beating her daily and determinedly, for centuries, to make her vanish, but she refuses to go away'. Truth is a very stubborn lady.

Concerning questions of a man's action: "first, whether it were done, or not done; secondly, if done, whether against the law, or not against the law; the former whereof, is called a question *of fact*; the latter a question *of right*."[22]

Think a moment. Why is an action investigated in such a case? Precisely because it is an action suspected of being legally wrong. The value occasions and constitutes the 'fact'. The word *fact* in that seventeenth-century use means "an action, something done" (a strong etymological meaning of the word, from *factum*, thing done), particularly a criminal act, and one can see something of perhaps how more modern meanings came to be: an act, and a judgment about the action — to — a fact (in other senses) and judgment, evaluation of fact.

"Want the facts? Want to learn the truth about prominent personalities?" 'What sort of facts?' 'Oh, you know, such facts as that Rebecca West had a 'love child' by H. G. Wells [Was the love a fact? Do these two deserve in fact better company than the issue gives them?], that it will cost Jane Fonda a 'pretty penny to drop her husband' and that she is 'regarded [in Hollywood] as a woman of intelligence . . . breeding, and civic-mindedness' and that Christopher Reeve is 'shacked up' with a British model.'[23]

"*FACT*: We can help you write better term papers." One way is by the use of "Pre-Written Research Studies" (that is, finished term papers). Is it a fact that buying and copying a term paper is *writing* a term paper? Are such term papers better term papers? Are they term papers at all? In fact?[24]

A title, "Health: Facts & Fallacies,"[25] makes it clear that facts are not — and perhaps cannot by definition be — fallacies.

"The standard of excellence as a guide to essential facts."[26]

Are the facts excellently essential?

A frequently used phrase is "the facts in dispute." Haven't we heard that facts are indisputable, firm, positive truth? Yet we often say that facts are disputed. For they are.

"Facts. . . the simple data of science."[27]

"Men of science have as their aim the discovery of facts."[28]

Is the whole aim of science to get the simple data it needs to begin with? Can't even scientists get their facts straight?

"Our graph modifies an assumption which *may* be correct, that one of our 'facts' is perhaps open to question."[29]

Was the fact a fact until the possible new evidence, and then did the fact become a 'fact'?

"Though the development of scientific ideas is, like everything else, a process of continuing change, which can never be absolutely complete, we can draw intellectual strength from the very fact."[30]

It is a relief to learn what a very fact is, since I was getting puzzled about what simple (non-very?) facts are.

"The undoubted fact that. . . it [the modern scientific world view] is an extremely anthropocentric world picture."[31]

There are scientists eager to doubt that undoubted fact.

"There is, at least in this age of science, almost complete unanimity as regards the criteria by which we judge the claims of ordinary factual knowledge."[32]

"The criterion of factual meaningfulness has been the issue of intense disputes for more than twenty years."[33]

"The romantic trappings of myth are belied by the prosaic facts. Charles Peace was, in truth, a conscienceless, mendacious villain, a lecher, a moral monstrosity."[34]

It's good to learn what the prosaic facts quietly are.

"But," remonstrated Watson, "the romance was there. I could not tamper with the facts."[35]

That, quite typically, is gracious of Watson. For the fact-proclaimers have been tampering with romance and other values for a long time. What is valuable is nonetheless valuable.

In plain truth, the concept 'fact' won't do. It is emotive of confidence, yet claims to be non-emotive. It is extremely entangled and vague of meaning yet claims to be clear.

It might be replied that the problems come from non-scientists using the term. 'Keep off our property! No Trespassing by Amateurs!' My examples suggest considerable unclarity in the use of the term by scientists; nonetheless, if the word were or had been restricted to mean only 'scientific truth', the problems would be fewer. But in that case why use the word at all? Why not just say "truth" or "reality" or "true statements" or the like? Because such words open metaphysical questions and truths which the word *fact* hides or begs?

The concept 'fact' won't do.

Nonetheless it stubbornly and ingrainedly attracts. It's hard to let go of. 'Ah, what a relief! we can know that; it is a fact.' Wishful thinking is not confined to one party of believers.

Men hunger for truth, a metaphysical hunger and not merely a pragmatic one. God always seeks for us, in our very fleeings from Him. It is good to know. It is good not to be deceived. It really is, and what scientist — when not shoving on a philosophical hat that does not fit — would deny it? Therefore the very search for facts (truth) is rooted and grounded in value,[36] and the dichotomy of fact and value is, at its very basis, false. One is deceived if he restricts truth to fact, and fact to shiftings.

'What is truth? Only science can tell. Can science tell about moral truth, truth of value? No.' Then there is no value (at least that we can tell about), and therefore we can never claim any value for science. Science is, like everything else, worth-less, intrinsically and instrumentally.

But science is worth much, intrinsically and instrumentally. Something has gone wrong.

To explore what, I shall turn next to two examples, looked at in some length, from two admirable works of careful scholarship.

Hyder Edward Rollins's Variorum edition of Shakespeare's sonnets is one of the greatest helps any student of Shakespeare's sonnets has, a tremendous labor which sums, with care and perception, an astonishing amount of scholarship. The irony and wit, aimed at scholarship gone awry or speculatively absurd, are enjoyable and no doubt helped their wielder through his enormous task. In the wit and elsewhere appear a conjoining of a love for poetry with a good share of scepticism and positivism.

Poetry is good; and aesthetic criticism is admirable: Rollins puts these across some magic wall immune from harm. On the other side of the wall, disagreement seems to prove the insolubility of problems, and the only kind of scholarship which is justified is that which put things "out of doubt" by getting the "facts."

At the end of the section on the rival poet he writes, "However gratifying it may be to a scholar or a critic to identify this man or that as the rival poet,. . .he can hardly expect everybody else to approve of his theorizing unless some biographical document. . .turns up to put the matter out of doubt."[37]

By the same argument, one can hardly expect everybody to approve of Rollins's procedural theorizing which accepts only the documented and out of doubt. Degrees of probability are matters of judgment, and lesser degrees than certainty may not automatically be equally scorned.

Some truth in what Rollins says is plain: it is always good to have evidence solid enough to settle a question. But having "everybody. . .approve" does not constitute truth. People can agree and be wrong. Virtual unanimity obtains on the authenticity (the authorship by Shakespeare) of the bulk of the sonnets; Rollins himself shrewdly shows that the case had not, prior to 1944, been established by argument.[38] Agreement and clearly evidenced truth are not coterminous.

Nor does disagreement prove the impossibility of knowledge. When men disagree, some can be wrong, some right; all can be wrong; some men argue better than others; men can argue poorly and be right; and so on. It does not follow from disagreement that the right course is to hold no opinion, a course which, followed, would cancel out very nearly all religious, political, and moral beliefs. In one of his smiling and charming asides Rollins writes, "Who shall decide, when doctors disagree?"[39] But one thing doctors disagree about is what to do when doctors disagree. Who shall decide? Each must, as he may.

Sceptics would like to stand on the sidelines and observe the game; but they are in a game where there are no sidelines. Play it we shall; we are there.

At the beginning of his discussion of the possible date or dates of the 154 sonnets in the edition published in 1609, Rollins summarizes

many theories and opinions concerning the question of date. After a
wearily jovial compilation of "rout on rout" of opinion, he writes, "It
is unnecessary to say that the date of composition is altogether
doubtful."[40] Even on his own summing, the consensus is not altogether
doubtful, since the majority of the scholars he sums agree that most
of the sonnets were written in the 1590s. Nor should the lack of a
consensus prove that one should withhold judgment. Not all quarrels
are ties; not all uncertainties are equally uncertain. If quarrels were
ties and uncertainties equally uncertain, then we should (assuming
"should" could make any sense in such a world) withhold judgment
on all or almost all matters whatever. People disagree about many
things.

Nor are facts the key. People disagree very widely about how the
facts work in given instances, what the facts mean, and — as the
examples already gathered show — what facts are. To say that facts
are clearly knowable, verifiable, supported by wide consensus, as
opposed to values, depends on what examples are chosen. Clear cases
for facts, the hard cases for value. Many values are very widely agreed
on, many 'facts' in elaborate dispute or uncertainty.[41]

Peter Geach writes, "it is an error in method in moral philosophy
to concentrate on what is problematic and disputable rather than study
the methods of reaching agreement. . . . there may be irresoluble
disagreements about matters of fact; observation, memory, and
testimony are all fallible. For an instance of this, we need only consider
a legal wrangle about a traffic accident: people will dispute about just
what happened, and also about what would have happened if suitable
avoiding action had been taken; and there is no decision procedure
for reconciling such disputes."[42]

Note that the second example of fact Geach gives, "what would
have happened if. . ." is a fact in relation to value, created by value:
what would have happened if *better* choices had been made. Note, even
more firmly, that the whole investigation and noting of fact as well as
value comes from the decision to find out what *damage* was done and
who should be *responsible*. Factual situations are value-grounded and
value-laden. Always.

Again, what is fact? Rollins has a view. He writes, of the question
of the date of composition of Shakespeare's sonnets, "A few facts are
available, even if their significance has been continuously debated."[43]

By facts he mean (1) the reference by Francis Meres in *Palladium Tamia*, published in 1598, to Shakespeare's "sugred [sugared] sonnets among his priuate [private] friends"; (2) the appearance of Sonnets 138 and 144 [by the numeration in the 1609 edition] in *The Passionate Pilgrim* in 1599; (3) the entry in the Stationer's Register in 1600 "A booke called *Amours* by J. D. with *certen* . . . sonnetes by W.S." [italics in text]; (4) Thomas Thorpe's license procured on May 20, 1609 to publish the sonnets; (5) Edward Alleyn's June 19, 1609 diary, noting that he bought "a book. Shakesper sonetts" for five pence.[44]

Very strictly considered. there are no facts; there are only truths. The word *fact* is, as has been shown, a word of vapid and highly polemical meaning, considering how precise it sounds and considering the firmness it is meant to exhibit. There are truths; there is evidence; there is more and less rationally or otherwise justified belief; but there is no realm where facts sit safely and neatly apart from theory or speculation or evaluation. Rollins's five 'facts' are relevant exhibits.

The five items listed are genuine; that is, I believe because I have good evidence (eye-witness, direct or of a transcript, for the first four; on good authority, Rollins's, for the fifth) that Meres said that, that the two sonnets do appear in the 1599 book, that the Stationer's Register said what it did about *Amours* and Thorpe's license; that Alleyn's diary referred to the book and its price.

But if one means by *fact* what is often meant, a clearly evidenced statement about something in the physical world ("it's a fact that the window is open now"), then it is odd to use the word *fact* to speak of what someone wrote. Further, if we mean by "available facts" facts available about the sonnets of Shakespeare and plainly relevant to dating the sonnets, which is clearly what Rollins intends, then Meres's reference to the sugared sonnets and the Stationer Register reference to "sonnetes by W. S.," may not concern the 1609 sonnets at all.[45] Meres may refer to other sonnets, fourteen-line poems, by Shakespeare or to short poems which are not fourteen-line poems, a common meaning of *sonnet* at that time. "W. S." may very well not be Shakespeare, since many men shared those initials. Either reference may be to the sonnets of Shakespeare, but *may* and *fact* do not cohere. One cannot rationally insist on good sound relevant facts as against speculations. judgments, and such, when the 'facts' are only possibly true and relevant.

Further, in Rollins's context "fact" plainly means a truth about what is in a text. By such a meaning, internal evidence becomes as much or little factual as the presumably hard external evidence. It is thus a fact that in line 14 of Sonnet 13 the speaker says to a young man, "You had a father; let your son say so." It is also a fact (that is, a virtually incontestable truth) that in ordinary modern usage the idiom "you had a father" means that the father is dead, the idiom "you have a father" means that the father is alive. The significance and interrelationships of these truths is debatable: the poem may not be biographical, the idiom may be used in a non-modern or non-normal sense, and so on. But by the inferable meaning of *fact* as used by Rollins, internal evidence is peculiarly factual and in any event as trustworthy as much external evidence. In my judgment, it is more likely that two of Shakespeare's sonnets were written by 1599 than that the young man's father was dead, but more likely that the young man's father was dead than that the "certen . . . sonnetes by W. S." refers to some or all of the 1609 sonnets.

A will, a signature, a title page, a letter, a public record, or a diary is not a poem; each has its uses for scholarship; none is infallible. The distinction between the comparative value of external and internal evidence usually depends on highly selective exemplification. Samuel Schoenbaum writes that a "chief limitation of [Leslie] Hotson's later work . . . is his proneness to attach the same evidential significance to a literary inference (say, the interpretation of an ambiguous topical allusion) as to an irrefutable documentary discovery."[46] Indeed so, and tautologously so. What is irrefutable is irrefutable. Only what of an irrefutable literary inference (that Shakespeare was moody or that his metrical style is more complex than Daniel's) and a highly ambiguous documentary discovery? Schoenbaum says of a possible detection of Hotson's, "One fact alone give us pause, and that is the ordinariness of the name John Jackson."[47] Some documentary evidence is very ambiguous. Evidence is evidence, and various; we judge as we may.

Selective exemplifying invades the presumed distinction between fact and value. Facts are felt to be solidly known, value typically dubious, because of the examples chosen or vaguely imagined.[48] But there is often more disagreement about fact than about value. There is far more agreement about the value in general of Shakespeare's sonnets and even about which poems and groups of poems are the better ones (though there is a fair amount of disagreement there) than about what people, if any, the sonnets concern. The value of the *Iliad* is agreed on; its unity of authorship is not. The value of *Peri Hupsous* (*On the Sublime*) has been asserted by romanticist and neoclassicist alike. Who "Longinus" was, when and where he lived (1st Century AD and 3rd Century AD are both supported), and even his actual name, are uncertain.

It is certain (probability of 1.0) that Shakespeare had great poetic talent, a judgment of value; it is quite uncertain what he had for dinner, if anything, on August 5, 1591, a question of solid and liquid fact. I respectfully request anyone who thinks these examples are frivolous or special pleading, to reflect a while. If value is not real, neither facts nor science can have value.

In general, it is an illusion based on a highly selective choice of examples that fact is solid and agreed-on, value vague and problematic. It takes a complex process (mis-process) of abstraction away from our experience to separate fact and value; it is only after establishing, by logical violence, a value-free world as reality, that one can wonder how to get from fact (is-statements, descriptions) to value (ought-statements, evaluation). We are already there, in the world and in truth.

J. A. Montgomery writes in "The New Sources of Knowledge" in *Record and Revelation*, the following:

"The advance of science records not only the discovery of new facts but also the explosion of old theories. There is a famous Palestinian coin, for a long time in the British Museum, presenting a male divinity seated on a wheeled chariot, holding a hawk in his hand, with an accompanying Hebrew legend which was read 'Yahu'. The natural conclusion was that here is proof of the eclectic assimilation of the God of the Jew with pagan deities. Professor Cook gives it the title, 'Yahu as a solar Zeus'. But Dr. E. L. Sukenik has now, with the assistance of two recently discovered coins, correctly diagnosed the legend as *yhd*, i.e., *Yahud*, the Aramaic form of *Yehuda* = *Judah*. He thus establishes the fact that Judea had its provincial coinage under the Persian empire."[49]

What here is fact, what theory? That Judea had its provincial coinage under the Persian empire, a historical generalization subsuming many

people and many coins, is, we are told, an established fact, a fact of
comparable generality to the now-exploded theory of the eclectic
assimilation of the God of the Jews with pagan deities. Yet the theory
is disproven by a re-reading of fact: the letters on a single coin,
interpreted. The once-fact, now non-fact, ex-fact, of the reading
"Yahu" is replaced by the new, established fact of the reading y[e]h[u]d.
The old fact is as exploded (if it is) as the old theory. Facts and theory
stand together, tremble together, fall together.

One may say, 'but such facts aren't really facts, but interpretation'.
Very well, then, what facts are there without interpretation? and how
probably established does an interpretation of evidence have to be
before it can count as fact? Were we to limit the word *fact* to the
practical certitude of such physical truths as an open window, the
word's use would be radically narrowed from its actual usage. And,
even with the open window, only those in the room at the time could
agree to the fact; those not in the room could not say validly, 'It is an
observable fact that. . .', but only such things as 'John reports that it
was to those in the room at a specific time an observable fact that. . .'
And even the open window, to those in a room at a given time, won't
entirely behave, since it after all can be contended about. How far up
or out does a window have to be to count as open? Someone might
contend that window which opened out was open, but that a raised
window should not be called 'open' but 'raised'. And so on. The
statement about the fact could be a joke, lie; the appearance of openness
could be part of a magic trick. Even the plainest facts waver, when
hassled. Human contention is limitless of possibility.

Does the notion 'fact' entail or require certitude, probability (how
much?), certainty beyond mere certitude, what? And what of the fact
(the reading *Yahu* and the corresponding interpretations, for instance)
that cease to be facts? Were they really facts to begin with, or only
semblances, illusions of facts? But, if so, can the new facts be called
fact? Is a fact only and truly a fact when it cannot be overthrown? If
so, facts become few. If not, what becomes of the confidence in fact?
And, to stir an overlapping issue, does science advance whenever
scholars disagree?

The word *fact* does shift, its claim to plainness is unearned. It can
mean "truth,"[50] almost innocently if usually a little flattened. The
word *truth* has a metaphysical glow (has and — thank God — should

have); the word *fact* has a metaphysical twist downward, variously realized in varying degrees, hinting of mere collocation, practical limits, nuts-and-bolts, debunking, devaluing. It suggests both practical value and no value ('it's useful to know the facts'; 'description is not evaluation') with an inconsistency that hides and sometimes distorts. It suggests plainness, yet is obscure; it smacks of the impersonal, the 'objective', the non-emotive, the carefully procedured, yet its main meaning — the one that most links the various meanings this chapter has pursued — is the felt confidence of the speaker who uses it. Most of all, it in much of its use insinuates value out of reality, without argument.

Fact won't do. Evidence and truth and reflection will.

Behind the notion 'fact' is a monistic impulse to reduce.[51] The drive of monism is strong, in epistemology as well as elsewhere, and to abandon monism too easily is to sail away into some vanishings (deconstructed vanishings, some of them). 'There are many points of view; all have much to recommend them; we should be tolerant; we really can't at all tell'. (Then we cannot tell whether we should be tolerant or not.) An ease of relativism slips seamlessly into the most despairing of scepticisms. The love of truth is a great virtue, greatly to be upheld, in faith and in science. The Catholic Church has wisely rejected the doctrine of Double Truth, which would save the Faith at too easy and in the long run much too high a cost. Yet there are multiple ways of coming at truth, of finding truths, and the premature attempt to unify them all (usually by dismissing the ways not favored) is also a disservice to truth. Not too forced a unity or too easy a multiplicity. Here, as elsewhere in our labors, we should neither despair nor presume.

The drive toward fact is very like the drive to reduce all knowledge to religious (Biblical) knowledge, an attempt, famously failed, which made for bad science and bad Scripturology, and severely discredited Biblical Revelation in many minds. It is easy now to condescend, a pleasure to be indulged with some caution. 'How could those foolish people be so conventional as not to share our conventions?' is a frequent and conventional question. An act of historical imagination is relevant. Men inferred as they inferred, for reasons.

'Can God's Truth lie?'

'No, but our interpretations, even our recordings, even our scriptural recordings and interpretations, can err'.

'Surely one can infer from the Word of God, from truths spoken by Truth, other truths, about many things'.

'Well, no, not really, not like that. Truth is not that simple. And that's not what the Bible is for. Through the Bible God reveals God and Christ'.

The inferences were made, 4004 BC was promulgated as the date of creation; and then the rocks were shown to be older, very much older; and conflicts soared, monism against monism, in murky light.

For someone who believes, as I do, that God is the Creator of time, the question, 'When did God make the world?' is an ill-formed question not capable of an answer, implying what God did not and has not created time. Put another way, "4004 BC" and "aeons ago" are equally valid answers. A better answer is 'Tomorrow', since it might startle forth some truth.

Bertrand Russell discusses with amusement the attempt to reconcile the evidence by saying that God created the world in 4004 BC as though it had a past history.[52] Suppose one were to take that seriously, in some real sense, not only for that one inferred occasion but for every occasion. God creates the world now with its past; God shall create the world tomorrow with its past; God creates the past then and always. That is, the view that God's Creation is eternal, hence (so to speak) perpetual, gives a better and less puzzling state to the past than the past has in most of our thinking or presuming. All things remain in God, including the past.

The world-daters were wrong, but are at least in logically better shape than the thinkers that argue that all thought is simply physiological or, more modestly, that thought may well be proved someday to be entirely physiological. If such a thought were true, it would instantly vanish (no need for further research) from being the thought it is. Even were it to be argued that thought is the brain's immediate self-consciousness, one needs to comment, first, that the notion of the brain's consciousness is a transfer which does not illuminate the mind-body question at all (it merely restates it); and, second, even if such a phrase (with lots of physiological data — all the physiological data — tossed in) made sense, the thought would still be logically and inescapably distinct from the consciousness that held it.

The drive of monisms is powerful, metaphysically powerful, and can be noble. The drive to unify our knowledge is hardly a trivial human aim. But monisms, including the positivistic, empiricistic one, do not reach and hence have a strong tendency to distort the evidence to make it fit. Hardly a scientifically creditable enterprise. As in horsemanship and good literary theory, the horse needs the spur and the reins. The doctrine of the Trinity should warn the Christian who thinks, and perhaps even be an impressive limit and analogy to non-Christians, that the problem of the one-and-the-many is not going to be solved by us. Ever. (The problem may vanish, when we see.)

The term *sub-atomic particles* (as handsome a self-contradiction as the term *free verse*) is a testimony to a monism gone wrong. The atom the basic unit? Hardly so. Lucretian atomism of long ago has not been borne out in detail by scientific investigation, but was a potent guess and in some ways a correct foretelling.[53] Did it reduce all to atom? No, to void and to atoms (plural) with distinct and different shapes, in motion, swerving, in relation to each other, in space and time.[54] Void, atom, number, shape, relation, motion, space, time are at least eight and can rapidly be multiplied beyond (the numbers of the many atoms, the subclasses of shapes, the special atoms of the soul and of the gods).[55] Monism is like that. Parmenides offers a perfect and motionless sphere, on negating arguments of some impressiveness:[56] what is in change is surely in some sense unreal, unrealized, transient and defective of being. Yet the illusion that there is other, even if it is mere illusion, is itself still one other than the One. Physicalism and Idealism shall be discussed later in this book in relation to subject-object bifurcating. Behaviorism is a halfway house on wheels, a mobile home, the mind-and-body puzzles hid in various cupboards and laundry chutes within.

The concept 'fact' is in good measure, I am arguing, the product, a shadowed and shifted product, of a strong monistic drive to reduce the world to conceptually and procedurally manageable matter-of-fact.[57] The world does not reduce, so, not even when scientifically grasped. For instance, biology requires teleology, in small and large ways.

Such a monism, though, has its comforts as well as its distortions. It is *good* to know on evidence; it is good to extrude what is partial and distorting in our desires from observation and thought; scientific discipline, imagination, and strong and changing methods, have impressively achieved. Instrumentally, science has produced and made possible much good and much evil. One cannot consistently praise science for its good consequences and then say of the evil results that science and scientists have no responsibility for the consequences. Science is intrinsically good, since to know is the good of the mind. But to claim for it exclusiveness of result or method (many scientists to their credit do not) is unjust to the evidence and would whittle much of reality away, including the value of science. The word *fact* reflects and perpetuates something of the complexity of that history. Insofar as it reflects a need for sound evidence carefully applied, it reflects a good, though the term is itself not carefully and evidentially applied. But, insofar as the usage of the term distorts and hinders our vision and would dissolve, by a gramatical dance, value, it deserves the complaint this chapter is.

2

Where Is Value?

What is-statements and ought statements are and what their relations are, is very far from clear (the question "Is yo' is or is yo' ain't my baby?" drifts nearby), and the base of the accusation of the 'naturalistic fallacy' is a truncated view of nature (reality), which among other things begs the essential questions at issue. When one defines or presumes 'nature' to exclude all value, to be only that which admits of pure value-free description, one indeed has a problem reading any value back into such a nature as defined or presumed. Remove the definition, and the problem vanishes. Reality and language are value-rich, and every move of language is value-founded, value-presuming, value-laden, and intended to realize value. To the is-ought question and the 'naturalistic fallacy' I shall later return.

This chapter is primarily a discussion of a famous passage in David Hume. Hume wished to be considered a man of discerning, delicate, and accurate taste, and he thought of himself more as a man-of-letters than as a philosopher. He therefore hardly wished to undercut ethics and artistic judgment, and in truth was in *A Treatise of Human Nature* trying to justify ethics and literary taste within a philosophic view of a empirical world not admitting ethical or aesthetic qualities. His strategy, roughly but I think basically, was to find that value resided only in human emotions but that human emotions have a basic, universal structure in mankind (eccentricities and distortions being purifiable by study, reflection, reading and good models), so that essential agreement in ethics and artistic judgment can be reached. That such a strategy has not worked historically is manifest, and has its philosophical liabilities. But *le bon David* was not aiming to be a foe to virtue and taste. Nor am I primarily discussing or directly concerned with the question of what Hume's later or final position on such issues,

17

is. The passage is famous, a historic landmark in the segregation of value from fact, and often quoted with approval. The issues are my concern.

In Hume's psychology in the *Treatise,* reason is "perfectly inert," "utterly impotent" to "produce any action,"[1] and reason can affect action indirectly, by making errors in matter-of-fact which mislead the emotions to urge a mistaken action. Only the emotions produce action.

Reason is the discovery of truth and falsehood, which consist in agreement or disagreement either "to the *real* relation of ideas, or to *real existence* and matter of fact."[2] All reason, then, is either comparing of ideas or inferring of matter of fact. But it is "allow'd on all hands, that no matter of fact is capable of being demonstrated,"[3] hence if reason is to infer anything about morality, it must do so by comparing real relations. But reason cannot do so, because trees commit parricide (kill by outgrowing and overshadowing their parent trees) innocently and animals commit incest innocently, but if the morality consisted in those relations, the trees and animals would be guilty. To the objection that men act knowingly and willingly (i.e., have choices) and trees do not, he replies that that affects only the causes of the action, not the real relations.

He further holds that "passions, volitions, and actions" have "no reference to other passions, volitions, and actions," and consequently cannot be "true or false" or "either contrary or conformable to reason."[4]

The psychology is hardly satisfactory. I would like to point to one extremely important word: "to" in the phrase "no reference to," since it implies that passions can have no reference to any action whatever.

The passage follows:

"But can there be any difficulty in proving, that vice and virtue are not matters of fact, whose existence we can infer by reason? Take any action allow'd to be vicious: Wilful murder, for instance. Examine it in all lights, and see if you can find that matter of fact, or real existence, which you call *vice.* In which-ever way you take it, you find only certain passions, motives, volitions and thoughts. There is no other matter of fact in the case. The vice entirely escapes you, as long as you consider the object. You never can find it, till you turn your reflexion into your own breast, and find a sentiment of disapprobation, which arises in you, towards this action. Here is a matter of fact; but 'tis the object of feeling, not of reason. It lies in yourself, not in the object. So that when you pronounce any action or character to be vicious, you mean nothing, but that from the constitution of your nature you have a feeling or sentiment of blame from the contemplation of it. Vice and virtue, therefore, may be compar'd to sounds, colours, heat and cold, which, according to modern philosophy, are not qualities in objects, but perceptions in the mind."[5]

He goes immediately on to congratulate himself:

"And this discovery in morals, like that other in physics, is to be regarded as a considerable advancement in the speculative sciences; tho', like that too, it has little or no influence on practice. Nothing can be more real, or concern us more, than our own sentiments of pleasure and uneasiness; and if these be favourable to virtue, and unfavourable to vice, no more can be requisite to the regulation of our conduct and behavior."

'Act on our feelings; and all will be well'. 'Act on our feelings' is a neat summary of a major strand of romanticism; not all that has followed has been well. Moral subjectivism has had a very strong influence on practice, via moral doubt and consequent anomie, and via the ethics of Will, a large impact for ill. The passage is a watershed in history, and some of the consequent other-ward floods have been strong. The reason of the Enlightenment (itself fed by the long moral history, Faith, and reasoning of Christendom) is put by. Reason grants its own incompetence, proclaims itself "utterly impotent," and, with smiling, benevolent calm and self-congratulation, turns over the direction and navigation of our lives to the passions. History spoke in the words.

Since what he says *is*, in some significant ways, our modern world, since he speaks the concepts by which many modern persons see and mis-see their experience, it is almost tautology to say that his view has been highly persuasive to many people. Indeed it has.

Empiricists are fond of attacking metaphysics while claiming they have no metaphysics, but their ancestor Hume gives that move plainly away. "Matter of fact, or real existence" identifies fact as existence.

His view is metaphysical at the base, though, be it noted, a base which shifts about while concepts collide. He both says that reason can infer matter of fact and that reason cannot demonstrate matter of fact. Presumably a distinction is intended, perhaps (roughly) between induction and deduction respectively. Otherwise the inconsistency is blunt. But supplying such a distinction, does not suffice. Morality is disconnected from matter of fact as a consequence of the view that reason cannot demonstrate matter of fact. He fails to show, what is needed for his argument, that reason cannot infer (or induce) virtue and vice as matter of fact. His argument is crucially incomplete.

Moreover, it is inconsistent. He had excluded quite generally morality (virtue and vice) from being findable in matter of fact, but also finds that passions are matter of fact and that virtue and vice reside in the passions, which is, then, it would follow, in matter of fact.

Even more important, he insists that emotions have no reference to action, and therefore that emotions cannot be true or false, or conformable to reason. Yet, in the most crucial move of his argument, he says that the sentiment of misapprobation *to* the action called wilful murder is where the vice resides. His little word "to" makes it possible that the sentiment could be right or wrong and conformable to reason or not. Without the "to" his case does not work at all, for the sentiment of misapprobation then would be totally at random, utterly disconnected from the action of murder or any other action. With the "to," the actual world we inhabit can return; the prison door stands open.

The sentiment of misapprobation is an ingenious place to tuck the real world, and Hume deserves credit for trying to save morality from the metaphysics of empiricism. But the real world is too large for the pocket, and the attempt to tuck vitiates his argument: a sentiment of approbation is no longer a mere sentiment; it is a sentiment cognized, in which a judgment has entered. We feel disapproval towards things we disapprove of, approval towards things we do approve of, in good part because we have been taught what is right and because our emotions have responded. We do instruct our emotions, though — as we all only too well know — the instruction is imperfectly received by the students. (Like all lively students, the emotions instruct us too.)

Hume precisely excludes judgment — faithful and feeling and

reasoning judgment — which is what we very importantly do, and Hume's substitute counters cannot logically fit or get the work done.

To shift the moral reality to emotions of approval, or to approval, or to commendation (a more recent move) is just to get things backward. To say that what a judgment that an act is wilful murder means is that the judger on each such occasion feels a sentiment of misapprobation in his breast (and that is Hume's position) is observably wrong, since one can make the judgment and not happen to feel any emotion (or a different emotion than blame — perhaps sympathy or repulsion or both or a strong emotion without a name). To say 'I believe that murder is wrong because I feel an emotion of disapproval' or 'I believe that murder is wrong because I disapprove it' or 'I believe that murder is wrong because I discommend it' is stubbornly backward, a stubbornness that permeates much philosophy. What we should say, and do say when not shoving our 180⁰-twisted feet into philosophical shoes, is 'I feel an emotion of blame (sometimes) towards murder because I believe it wrong'; 'I disapprove of murder because I believe it wrong'; 'I discommend murder because I believe that murder is wrong'. 'Murder is wrong' is — grammatically and in reality — an is-statement of a very important kind about the real world. 'But we don't want the world that way', the empiricists in effect reply. 'We want the world stripped so that we can know it clearly, so that we don't have to fear it, so that we can control it, subject it to our understanding and will'. Yes, desire is powerful, and thus sometimes a hindrance.

In Hume's passage, the sentiment of misapprobation is towards an action. What action? Wilful murder? No. For, by Hume's account, the *action* is not wilful murder, or rather is not wilful murder until the sentiment of misapprobation which blames the action for being wilful murder, constitutes the action as wilful murder. A tangle of logical knots in a twisting. And it isn't so.

To say "I commend something" and "I do not believe it to be really good" is not only inconsistent, but in most instances hypocritical. When a scholar commends a book he believes to be a bad book, he obviously is telling an untruth. And if one feels a strong emotion of blame towards something one does not judge to be wrong (and thus blameworthy), something needs straightening out, the feeling or the judgment. Or both could be awry.

Yet the Humean subjectivists, and at least many prescriptivists (commend-ers) are perpetually in that inconsistency, of feeling approval toward, or commending, and not believing that the action (or whatever) one feels approval toward or commends, is actually good. And in a like inconsistency for blaming and discommending. The solution is very simple, and very hard to apply, because one is up against centuries of torsion, of attempts to strip the world of value in order to know it better (more valuably — an inconsistency at the very root of empiricism), attempts which have bent our language toward (but not to) the forcers' will.

Some time ago, we are told, the Tempter tempted by saying, "eat thereof . . . ye shall be as gods, knowing good and evil."[6] More recently he has shifted tactics, saying 'you cannot be as gods, knowing good and evil', evasively intending both 'you cannot know good and evil *as* gods know good and evil, with godly certainty' and 'you cannot, in ordinary and important human senses of *know*, know good and evil at all, because there really isn't any good and evil'. The crop of tares? Despair, scepticism, wilfulness, including the curious wilfulness of choosing one's values, deciding what moral prescriptions one shall prescribe. (An effective move, but, thank God, the end is not yet.)

The section in Hume, inbreathing and furthering its milieu, defines and presumes value out of existence. Though he says, and means "Examine it in all lights," he looks with a very special blind lantern, which misses the world.

The psychological process he describes does not normally, if ever, happen. When one reads in a newspaper than an act of arson is suspected, one does not carry on some such internal dialogue as the following: 'Hmm. Arson. What reality does that involve? The action is merely setting fire to a building, on purpose, for profit. That's all that happened last night, if the suspicion is right. Well, then, how do I feel about it? Let me open a window to my breast and look within. What do I see? A good many goings on. Which one is relevant? Oh, yes. There, tucked under a pleasure for bacon just consumed and a remembered shame which (never mind), ah, yes, there it is! A sentiment of misapprobation. Ah, is it connected and relevant? [On strict Humean grounds one cannot ask that question: it occurs in a territory of reasoning not on his map and in his psychology emotions cannot refer to anything.] Ah, yes, the sentiment is *to* the incident last night. So I'll say (though not really mean) that the action was legally and morally

wrong and, now, I can call it arson'. Again, on Humean premises you
cannot truly call the act that happened, arson, since that implies that
the wrong is 'out there', that the action is wrong. But the vice resides
in the sentiment. Why, one might reasonably ask, does that not make
the sentiment vicious and the act innocent? How oddly cruel to impose
evil on an innocent (and valueless) world.

A judgment that arson is wrong is a judgment that arson is wrong;
it is not something in a feeling that accompanies and is occasioned by
the judgment. Even if one begins with the feeling, one has to go back
to the action being judged, for that is what the feeling (judgment)
concerns. A sentiment of misapprobation is a disapproval of something,
a judgment that some action is wrong. That's what misapprobation
means; that's how the language works.[7] But Hume cannot say so,
because he is stuck with (and proud of), at least on that occasion, his
empiricist view of reality and he wants to save virtue and judgment
and artistic excellence. The attempt does not reach.

He says that "Vice and virtue . . . are not qualities in objects." The
notion of qualities in objects has misled seeking for a long time. If one
says that virtue and vice have to be invisible qualities in 'objects' in
addition to everything in our analysis and judgment of an act, one
would think they would be hard to find. Suppose one judges, 'His act
was an act of arson and therefore wrong. He showed contempt for
innocent lives; he cared nothing about the people who might be hurt
in consequence, specifically the firemen; he was attempting to defraud
the insurance company. That's enough to show that his act was bad'.
Then does one, in addition, have to discover some very special quality
other than the whole act and the arguments you offer in order to show
the act wrong? The vice is not some exceedingly peculiar property in
the act, but the act itself: arson, a morally wrong act. The 'quality' has
vanished; it was never there. Nor are such qualities needed in order
for us to make valid judgments. Arson is an act which is really wrong;
one really should not do such acts.

"The vice entirely escapes you as long as you consider the object."
That's false in his paragraph; he is attending to the action not because
actions, volitions, and passions happened at random but because the
action is wilful murder. He says so: "Take . . . wilful murder for
instance." Wilful murder is precisely what he is attending to, studying,
and discussing. *That* action.

A newspaper account of arson attends to the act as an act of arson. Newspapers do not have reporters list at random "passions, motives, volitions, and thoughts" encountered in a city. They focus attention according to judgments (good, bad, or mixed) of what is significant in the events, what will realize the aims of the newspaper, including making a profit. One may debate the comparative excellence of the motives, but the motives are there: human enterprises are undertaken to realize ends (goods) and proceed by evaluating methods, situations, operations, and such. Human enterprises are in attempt value-realizing, including writing about philosophical issues. That frame, foundation, reality is normally ignored in discussion in moral philosophy; but it is what constitutes moral philosophy as other human action. Hardly a trivial truth.

Hume is trying to persuade readers of certain views in order to enlighten the readers and to realize his own ends: for instance, to achieve fame as a man of letters and as a philosopher. The enterprise is value-packed. At each breath, each quill stroke, he is presuming and trying to realize value, including the value of argument. He's not trying to stir and change the reader's emotions (say to approbation of him) by means of colored cartoons and pornographic asides and bells and perfumes. (Were he doing that, he would still be attempting to realize value.) But he is not. He is trying to persuade and analyze and clarify, to get the analysis and argument *right*. He is really trying to do that; he is not trying to slap together a botched-up argument which will happen to occasion in certain readers a sentiment of approbation-of-good-clear-rational-philosophizing or whatever. He is trying to do the argument well, to discover truth, to attain, in his own words, "a considerable achievement." What he is doing is inconsistent with the position he asserts, and really impossible even to describe within the strict and restricting confines of that position.

"When you pronounce . . . an action vicious . . . you mean nothing but that from the constitution of your nature you have a feeling or sentiment of blame from the contemplation of it."

People do not mean what Hume is saying they do when they pronounce an action vicious. They mean what they say, namely, that they are pronouncing the action vicious because they believe that the action is vicious. If they pronounce the action vicious but do not believe that it is vicious, they are lying, or perhaps philosophizing. Hume may mean that that is what people ought to mean, but then he should have said so. People can say what their feelings are (within some limits) and they can pronounce actions vicious. Hence, why think when they make one kind of statement they mean another kind of statement they can and frequently do distinguish? The distinction is plain enough: one can judge an action wrong while not at the same time having any particular kind of feeling about it. One can have a strong feeling of blame (or self-blame) for an action, but suspect that the feeling is irrational and not judge the action blameworthy.

The distinctions are there, which Hume missed; connections are there also, which he was banking on. For instance, we say when making judgments "I think that's such-and-so" or "I feel that's such-and-so," at times even interchangeably, though often with some difference of emphasis. Thought and feeling are both involved in making judgments, and we can stress either. When we call an action blameworthy, we conflate action, worth, and feeling (judgment). To blame is to judge, not merely to have a feeling. The concept *blameworthy* implies that feelings can fit actions. That feeling can be appropriate or inappropriate to reality. *One may appropriately feel blame for an action only when and because that action is wrong.* Hume's attempt to reduce all judgment to non-referential feeling and then to have the feeling refer back to the action is (1) self-inconsistent, (2) does not follow or explain the actual paths of the mind. He needs the determinedly reductive "nothing but"; and he needs more. For Hume in the *Treatise*, empiricism is truth; virtue is outside that 'truth'. What Hume is trying to do is, to vary a phrase of Yeats,[8] hold truth and virtue in a single thought (by tucking virtue into the feelings). It did not work, but was an elaborate try.

Hume ends, one is glad to say, on the other side from his famous passage. At least his autobiography so ends:

"To conclude historically with my own character — I . . . was . . . a man of mild disposition, of command of temper, of an open, social, and cheerful humour, capable . . . of great moderation in all my passions . . . I cannot say, there is no vanity in making this funeral oration of myself; but I hope it is not a misplaced one: and this is a *matter* of *fact* which is easily cleared and ascertained."[9]

Yes; moral judgment can be truth and proven sound.

3

The Truth of Value: Proofs and Examples

But how does one tell what moral and aesthetic judgments are right? How does one know? How does one know that there is truth of value? How would it be proved?

Such questions can be seriously asked and are therefore worth attention. This book has answered and will answer, will pluck away at knots, inspect real or (a harder job) inspect non-existent foundations, return, and return, and hope. One assumption wiggling within and beneath a woodpile of queries — the assumption that we can know, plainly, facts and that we cannot know value — has already been exposed and will be countered by many an example to come. Perhaps by sunset it will die. If so, it will doubtless prove a lively ghost.

This chapter will offer an example of moral judgment, the very widespread and agreed-on judgment that arson is morally wrong as well as illegal, in order to look at how moral judgments do work and to argue (or at least assert) that such judgments can be validated, known to be true. Then the argument shall be cast more generally.

The word and concept *know* provides its troubles, which become ours. It has its difficulty, as Wittgenstein pointed out, in bearing a metaphysical emphasis.[1] When we know, do we *know*, or are we just strongly convinced? Which raises the question of certainty.

In one sense the question is irrelevant. The thesis of this book is not that we can know aesthetic and moral truth with certainty or absolute certainty; the thesis of this book is primarily that there is better and worse moral and aesthetic judgment.

Nonetheless there are genuine senses in which we can say that we 'know with certainty' aesthetic and moral truths (some of them), as

27

well as other kinds of truth. If we mean that we have a firm conviction, good reason to believe, and no real reason to doubt, that we often have psychological certainty which we have a moral right to have, then we frequently know things with certainty. I am certain that I have enjoyed reading *Lycidas*; that I have fingers, that San Francisco is in California; that Robert Frost wrote some good poetry, that some cows have more than two legs; that lying is sometimes wicked; that arson is frequently morally wrong; and I am certain (so are we all) of a very great many other things. I can even say that I am absolutely certain of them, at least in some sense that makes "absolutely" pleonastic. If one is actually certain, one is actually certain. We really are sure; we have good reasons for being sure; we surely have a moral right to be sure; and to say that we are less than really sure would be to violate honesty.

If on the other hand 'know with certainty' means to know with absolute rational certainty, certainty perfectly sustained by demonstrative argument based on premises themselves rationally certain[2] (or whatever 'know with absolute certainty' may best mean —can we be certain of that?), then we may well not know anything at all with that kind of certainty. In a very severe Platonic sense of knowledge, we may well have no knowledge, only opinion. (I am not foreclosing the issue; I am not sure which is the right answer.) We are not angels but men. But that is another discussion.

What is important, in the polemics of this discussion, is that the defender of moral and aesthetic judgment not get caught in a crossfire between two senses of *know*, the opposition assuming that they can know or believe all sorts of things in the plain and ordinary sense of *know* and *believe*, while demanding that the defender of moral and aesthetic truth be required to take his stand on very high-uplifted standards of knowledge virtually out of sight. The question of certainty is in some ways germane, but not when infiltrated. Sauce the goose and gander alike.

Let us turn to the example. Why is arson wrong? How does one know? Note first that the moral wrongness of arson is much easier to establish and agree on (a question of value) than whether certain fires were actually caused by arson (a question of 'fact').

The illegality of arson does not automatically implicate its moral wrongness, but is good evidence for its moral wrongness, and very many people, including reflective people, would agree. Laws are passed against actions people believe to be wrong, actions against which they themselves and others wish to be protected. The protection of society, of people against fraud and violence, *is* good, and most people (all of the people some of the time) agree that such protection is good.

To say that laws and morals are merely for the convenience and protection of society, a frequent assertion of relativists, is non-relativistic: it presumes, as do the people being protected and convenienced, that the convenience of society is a distinct good, a *telos* worthy of achievement. That's the way the world is.

To argue in specific instances from law to morals is not infallible, but not foolish, and in the instance of arson a valid argument, for the legal reasons for objecting to arson are moral reasons; and — once more — this is a truth on which there is wide agreement.

We are apt to think of law and morality as separate realms. Yet the realms certainly overlap considerably (e.g., people pass laws against actions they believe wrong), and in one sense morality covers the whole realm of law, because any legal rule, edict, of whatever — depending on various considerations — *should* or *should not* be strictly enforced.

Legal positivism severs law and moral judgment absolutely, hence is clearly historically wrong. Further it is wrong on its own grounds, since the law itself includes requirements for moral reasoning, as in the concept of "reasonable man" and in the requirements that judges judge and modify some judgments on grounds of equity, of what they reflect on as right and wrong. Thus, if legal positivism is true, it is false. If it is false, it is false.

Historically law has been rooted in morality and religion, which is one reason that relativists are typically progressivists, so that they can reject the ties of nature and religion and law and morality as primitive concepts, myth, pre-rationalistic, pre-scientific, and such. But a progressivist cannot consistently deny value realism, for his position implicates it: things are getting *better*. "When me they fly, I am the wings."[3]

If positive law is the only law, what can legislators discuss? Should they not, if they wished to be rational, pass laws at random? Or should they revert to entire poll-ism, that is, no longer arguing in terms of what would be better and worse, but just voting as their constituents wish them to vote? But that in turn implicates a strong altruism, a loyalty to principles and constituents, and — once more — value. Then, if one waives judging right and wrong, each individual legislator could, in reason, serve his own ends by whatever means he saw fit: deceiving fellow legislators and constituents, and all. But that, in its own turn, would be realizing his ends, seeking a *good* for himself, fulfilling a *telos*, realizing value. But of course legislators do not legislate at random. They discuss and try to decide which laws would be better to pass. They do in practice, not only in ideal. That's what legislators are *for*, (their *telos*), and that is what legislators do, however much or little self-interest and muddledom warp their judgment. And to say that muddledom and self-interest warp, is to make a judgment, an evaluation. Language speaks in value. "When me they fly, I am the wings."

People disagree about laws; people do doubt specific laws, legal and moral. To doubt a legal law is to doubt its *value*, to doubt whether it is a good law. A fact-wielder may say, 'Yes, people do very often doubt whether laws are good ones, a highly disputable question of value. But the factual question of whether something is legal is easily settlable, by going to the laws of the appropriate state'. To which one may reply that it is not even easy to look up a law; it's hard for professionals and at times impossible for amateurs; being able to find a law amongst the many a state has passed is a developed skill, requiring application, diligence and other virtues. And it is just not true that the question what a law is, is cleanly and clearly settlable. What are law trials about? How many disputed questions are raised in law trials about how a law applies, about the interpretation of law (i.e., what a law is, what a statute says), or about the facts in dispute? The distinction between fact and value is a delusion, constantly reintroducing itself in trying to apply the concepts.

To doubt whether some law (moral or legal) is good is to imply that other laws may well be sound and to imply that there are reasons for doubting, that is, conceptual procedures for deciding. There is a great logical and structural difference between doubting some laws and doubting all. Doubt presumes knowledge and some hierarchy and connection of concepts. Universal doubt is not a manageable or thinkable concept.[4]

To try to undercut the value of all law, legal and moral, is to implicate, presume and assert value (and the morality of realizing value). To say something like 'There is no real ground for legal systems, and therefore they are not justified, do not refer to matter-of-fact or real existence' is to make a move in an argument, and argument is value-laden from start to finish. If no proof is offered, no proof is offered, and why should we believe? If a proof is offered, the presumption is the value of proof and the graspability of relevant conceptual structure. If an argument is valuable, that same argument by being valuable implies value. If an argument is not valuable, why should it be made? how could it be made? was the person who made it unmotivated, utterly without wish to realize some value? Further, the assumption that systems *should* be reality-based in order to be valid, is a moral and metaphysical assumption radically anti-sceptical. Take that assumption away, and the case for scepticism collapses. Grant the assumption, and the case for scepticism collapses.

What can seriously count, in any language-use whatever, for an argument which denies the stuff and texture of language and human experience? Language presumes value. Experience presumes value. Confusedly? Yes. That's why clarifying can be of value. We do not invent value; we experience it. In that sense, value-realism is experiential ('empirical') through and through.

The existence of law, and the social agreement therein implied, is a strong though not conclusive argument for the wrongness of arson. Nonetheless, waiving that and starting from scratch, what reasons can we give for arson's being wrong?

It is hardly difficult to give them.

Arson, when of another's property, is wrong because one has a duty not to destroy other people's property. It's not one's own. That's what *property* means, etymologically. One's own, is what properly belongs to one. The concepts of property and propriety are historically related because that relationship reflects thoughts and feelings and imagination and judgment made in our history. A man has earned his own property, by inheritance or labor; it has been contracted to him by others, hence it is his by promise. To burn his property violates his existence as a person, violates what he and other people did and agree. Other people actually exist and therefore obligate others, burden others even. We are not free to impose (put upon) other people. Their existence limits our action, in prudence and in right. They have dispositions toward good and harm, reasoning powers, imaginative capacities, are capable

of suffering and also of revenge. They simply are not mine — to use
or harm as I wish. They wish, too.If the property is one's own, then
one has no right to defraud others, by falsely collecting insurance and
raising insurance rates, endangering firemen. And so on.

Those arguments mingle legal, prudential, and principled
considerations — on purpose. Such are the ways moral reasoning
actually goes. The suggestion that one remove all such elements, strip
discourse utterly of value and evaluation, and then re-begin, is not
possible, desirable, or reasonable. One couldn't then say a word; the
first sentence would restore enough reality to cancel the condition.
(The fascination with beginning and re-beginning and not arriving, in
the poems of Wallace Stevens[5] and certain modern poetic theorizing,
is a germane and salutary warning.)[6] If one wants to get somewhere
he has to start where he is. No other way is known. And language,
reasoning, and judgment do implicate the reality of value, that is, the
genuine possibility of better and worse judgments. What is true within
our language and experience cannot be denied in language without
instant and perpetual self-inconsistency, for which the modern fondness
is well known and widely manifested.

A PROOF FOR THE REALITY OF AESTHETIC VALUE

The proof assumes a relation: that, if better and worse aesthetic,
moral or other evaluative judgment is genuinely possible, then value
is real. I believe that that relation is correct, that the premise implies
the conclusion, and it seems to me to be intuitively and overwhelmingly
evident, implied by "better," "worse," "evaluative," and "genuinely,"
severally and together. Much modern thought wishes to deny the
reality of value and yet to validate sound judgment (scientific, political,
and other). In my judgment, that task is doomed by inconsistency in
every move.

For a reader who severs judgment from the reality of value (however
coherent or incoherent his severing may be), the proof will be that
better and worse aesthetic judgment is genuinely possible. That,
however, is itself not trivial, since it contravenes much that much
modern poetic theory and practice states, implies, hints, or insinuates.

The proof is a transparently simple one. It is this: if the *Iliad* is a
poem of some poetic merit, then value is real; but the *Iliad* is a poem
of some poetic merit; therefore value is real. The premise is almost

comically mild. Its mildness is its strength. For the premise would still be true, if the *Iliad* were a preposterously bad poem with occasional and incidental poetic virtues. All one needs to maintain is that at least that much is true, that the *Iliad* does have at least some incidental poetic virtues. But, in truth, the *Iliad* is an overwhelmingly great poem of massive, sublime, and frequent excellences; and what is more, we know it: we have powerful and converging evidence for the greatness of the poem. Consequently the mild statement of the premise is about as certain as a statement can get, of the order of certainty of such statements as "some people have fingers." The premise makes sense, is true, and unmistakably is a judgment which is an evaluative judgment of a work of literature. The conclusion manifestly follows (assuming the relation already mentioned). Hence the argument does prove that aesthetic value is real, not a delusion, and that statements about it can make sense and be true. I realize that the locution "literary merit" can be quibbled with. So can any locution in any argument whatever. But the meaning is plain English and an educated reader knows what it means. Value, then, is real.

It may be objected that the argument is circular, since the premise "the *Iliad* is a poem of some literary merit" presumes the truth of the conclusion "aesthetic value is real." In asserting the notion "literary merit" I have asserted the notion I have wanted to prove. Not quite. I have mentioned the idea 'literary merit' and then given it an instantiation, namely the *Iliad*. If a value term we mention has a genuine instantiation, then the value term is thereby validated. Even if that is not granted, *use* and *mention* being tricky concepts, there is still no circularity that vitiates the argument. For if we know a statement to be true, we can infer statements entailed by the statement (including its presumptions) to be true. But we really do know (in a plain and ordinary sense of "know") that the *Iliad* is a poem of some literary merit. Therefore we can and must know (in a plain and ordinary sense of "know") that value is real.

It is often hinted or asserted that the trouble with literary judgment, or any judgment involving taste, is that there is no "evidence" for it. That view is not only false, but fantastic. There is excellent and widely known evidence for believing that the *Iliad* is a good poem. The truth that much or it is evidence that can be assessed only be a person capable of imaginative response does not damage its claim to be good evidence:

that is a rule for handling such evidence. To gather astronomical data with a telescope, one needs eyes. To see how powerful a poet Homer is, one needs to be able to respond to poetry. It is the crudest sort of epistemological mistake (which will cripple every form of knowledge, including the physical and biological sciences) to put epistemological demands on a subject that do not grow out of a particular and thoughtful exploration of the subject itself.[7] Feeling is a necessary condition of genuine literary knowledge — a statement for which the *evidence* is great.

A PROOF OF THE REALITY OF MORAL VALUE

If it is morally wrong to shoot children at random on a city street just for fun, then moral value is real. But it is morally wrong to shoot children at random on a city street just for fun. Therefore moral value is real. Or, less metaphysical sounding, the proof proves that one can make better and worse moral judgments. Someone who thought it was not morally wrong to shoot children at random on a city street just for fun would be making a moral mistake, and thus making a worse moral judgment than someone who disagreed with him.

The parallel to the aesthetic argument is deliberate, and the parallel to G. E. Moore's argument for the existence of an external world, namely, "Here is one hand and here is another" is not accidental, but is probably the result of influence of the Moore argument, via an argument by Renford Bambrough.[8]

There is, as I noted above, something that nears circularity in the argument, namely, that the premises are being used to establish presumptions of those premises. That is not vitiating, since if one accepts a statement as true one should accept its real presumptions as true. The logical connection is there.

The circle, if circle it is, cuts much more deeply. The argument really applies not just to those two statements, but to all discourse. All discourse proves the reality of value, because all discourse presumes the reality of value. That is what discourse is and does: it realizes values of various kinds, self-expression, fulfillment of a personal motive to realize some good for oneself, to speak truth (a good), to communicate to other people (that is, to commune with them, a good), whatever. Language is motivated and human, which is to say immersed in value, presuming value, value-laden, value-seeking, value-realizing.

A sceptic, momentary or confirmed, may doubt the reality of value, and may doubt the value of language, even though there is no way to *say* that doubt consistently, for to use language is to be public, human, value-intended, value-confirming.

Those doubts haunt modern poetics and related theorizing and billow the rhetoric thereof, but writhe as the words may,[9] at every turn the words deny the doubt, deny the scepticism, deny the deconstruction. And truly so. "When me they fly, I am the wings."

The chief problem in the fact-value dichotomy and in the is-to-ought puzzlings is that the very structuring of the dichotomies is invalid. One cannot ever say an is-statement, a pure and mere fact, in the sense intended: no statement is pure description, utter description, set free from all value, because statements *are* evaluations. The problem is not crossing the bridge from the is-statement to the ought statement. It's getting across the bridge in order to start with the is-statement. One cannot begin there, so there is no puzzle. The 'naturalistic fallacy' contains a fallacy all right, in the view-of-nature tucked into the word *naturalistic*, a nature that never was on land or sea, a nature that cannot be, a world of facts immune to all evaluation, and hence to all actual description. A nature that never was and cannot be said.

C. S. Lewis, in *The Abolition of Man*, a strong plea for belief in moral and aesthetic law, says, flatly, that the moral law's "validity cannot be deduced."[10] On the contrary, every deduction proves the existence of moral law, because deduction presumes the moral law: it presumes rationality, fairness as opposed to philippic, the treating of other people with respect, the value of truth, and the possibility of making deductions about truth.

I offer one more proof, by imperative: treat people as people because they are people. People are capable of being wounded; they can avenge; they have moral, spiritual, aesthetic, and other capacities which can be frustrated, worsened, or helped. Hence prudence and justice concur to support the argument.

People exist who attempt to use other people as instruments rather than as persons. (Some of them excel in sports or other activities — note the word *excel*.) It is impossible to do so wholly, since even the bad keep some sense of the real and the good. Still, some people make the attempt, in strong and ugly ways. In doing so, they inevitably bully or lie. That is, they use some form of force which they think will overcome the force of human nature, including the force of resentment, or they misrepresent what they do in order to deceive. Which is to say, that the manipulators in their very manipulation recognize and trade on basic moral truth about persons.

Another argument. If you doubt moral reality, get a job working closely with people for six months. You will *learn* the reality of value including moral relations and the reality of original sin.

4

Natural Law and Judgment

'But it's hard to arrive at general principles of morality and aesthetics. There are exceptions to rules'.

To say that general moral and aesthetic principles admit exceptions is to admit twice the thesis of the book, that one can make better and worse moral and aesthetic judgments. First, to say so is to imply that there are moral and aesthetic truths, that moral and aesthetic principles sometimes do apply to particular instances. Second, one asserts that there are exceptions to principles because one thinks of reasons for particular exceptions. One is, in arguing for any exception, making a moral or aesthetic judgment considered valid; one cannot then consistently deny the validity of moral and aesthetic judgments.

Are there universal principles which admit of no exceptions? In some ways, yes; but such principles are not the only principles that matter, nor can they be always easily and directly applied. Moral and aesthetic judgments do not consist exclusively of accurate and logically precise application of general principles to particular instances. Good judgment often requires the testing of principles against instances and vice-versa, with no formula in advance guaranteeing an exact and sure answer. Casuistry, the applying of principles to particular instances, requires judgment, and not all our thinking is done with propositions beginning with "All" or "Every."

To take a hypothetical example, suppose one knew, certainly, that 90% of acts of arson were wicked. Suppose further that one had no knowledge which specific acts of arson were wicked and that one had no way to determine which acts of arson were wicked. It would still be a strict obligation (assuming no other moral principles or considerations were applicable) to avoid every act of arson, since to commit any act of arson would probably be wicked.

The defense of value-realism does not, as such, logically necessitate a defense of natural law, if one means by "natural law" universal moral and aesthetic principles which do not admit exceptions. For it is logically conceivable that there could be no such principles (excluding — if it need be excluded — the metaprinciple that states there are no such principles) and that one could still make better and worse aesthetic and moral judgments. We get along fairly well by applying practical principles and knowing when they apply and when they don't. "Look before you leap" and "he who hesitates is lost" are both sound proverbs, though they cannot both be universal, since they are inconsistent. They are handy, and their inconsistency is not troublesome, since we know from experience examples and kinds of situations where each would apply.

Principles are tools of judgment. Judgment cannot do without principles, yet does not derivatively and tamely depend on principles. Judgment is not easy, but is, as Longinus said, "the last fruit of ripe experience."[1]

Principles test cases; cases, principles. For instance, Aristotle's notion of the tragic flaw[2] is a valuable concept in discussing and judging literary works, yet when applied to some works, for instance Shakespeare's *Macbeth*, causes problems. Either we have to say that *Macbeth* is not a tragedy of a very high order, because in the latter part of the play Macbeth is not a basically good character with a tragic flaw (as required by the theory) but a very bad man, a theologically-damnable tyrant; or we have to say that, since Macbeth is a tragedy of a very high order, the concept 'tragic flaw' is itself flawed. Or make other moves: for instance, reinterpret the concept or the play, or argue that the concept does not apply to that play.

One needs here, as frequently, the reminder that, while the hard instances get the attention — they are where the puzzles are, where the hard decisions are required — many, many instances of moral or aesthetic decisions are easy instances. Most instances of theft, for a citizen of at least moderate means, are just wrong. The instances that require no judgment are heartening, but easily overlooked in discussion.

People are good or at least loquacious at thinking up exceptions, finding border-line instances, reinterpreting terms or presumptions, and so on; and principles sometimes conflict: moral dilemmas occur; claims need to be weighed. Nonetheless, principles (rules) exists; they are necessary; and they frequently can be straightforwardly applied. The proponents of "situational ethics" tend to insist on the newness, the modernity of what they say; yet their primary notion, that judgments and decisions have to be made within contexts, has long been known and is what casuistry concerns.

PRIMARY AND SUBSIDIARY PRINCIPLES

Some principles are clearly more fundamental than others, hence governing in conflict and the basis for mediation and balancing. The gospel of Matthew tells us, after offering the Summary of the Law (to be quoted soon in this chapter): "On these two commandments hang all the law and the prophets."[3]

A close structural parallel in literary criticism occurs when Dryden, working within the Aristotelian and neoclassical tradition, distinguishes between primary and secondary principles. The "great foundation," the primary principle, is that poetry is an "imitation of nature."[4] Good poetry should be in accordance with nature, both as a representation (literature should have verisimilitude), and as something made, as a "*just and lively image*."[5] Poems should be vital, well-formed, appropriate, in accord with moral and aesthetic law and understanding, and with permanent and singular human nature; else they cannot long please. Other rules are secondary, of a lesser order of certainty, and therefore judgment, tradition, good sense, and mediation are permanent essentials of good criticism.[6]

Whether such neoclassical principles are accepted or not (I have argued elsewhere they are tacitly accepted and inescapably used by much criticism which rejects them in theory or ignores them),[7] or whether or not the highly useful distinction between primary and secondary is a simplified analysis, aesthetic or moral judgment requires principles, requires a sense of which principles are more fundamental, and is not (always) simply the automatic application of principles to particular works or situations.

The more fundamental literary or moral principles often require more interpretation than the secondary ones. The application of "Thou shalt not steal" is, in most instances, plain. "Thou shalt love thy neighbor as thyself " requires some judging to apply — faithful and thoughtful and loving judgment.

THE SUMMARY OF THE LAW AND THE GOLDEN RULE

The most general of moral precepts, the heart of natural law, has been given various formulations, yet keeps, if not an essence, a very close family resemblance. Some biblical formulations follow.

"Therefore all things whatsoever ye would that men should do to you, do you even so to them, for this is the law and the prophets." (Matthew 7.12, the Golden Rule)

"And as ye would that men should do to you, do ye also to them likewise." (Luke 6.31, the Golden Rule)

"Master, which is the great commandment in the law?

"Jesus said unto him, Thou shalt love the Lord thy God with all thy heart, and with all thy soul, and with all thy mind.

"This is the first and great commandment.

"And the second is like unto it, Thou shalt love thy neighbour as thyself.

"On these two commandments hang all the law and the prophets." (Matthew 22.36-40, summed from Deuteronomy 6.5 and Leviticus 19.18)

The "all thy mind" clearly lets us know that reasoning is required. A precept which includes the applying of it with all the mind, can hardly be a precept automatic to apply or a precept not to reason about. Nor can it be a precept that may be applied or entered or rejoiced in, by reasoning alone (all thy heart, all thy soul).

The second part of the Summary of the Law implies and goes beyond the precept 'Respect thy neighbor as thy self'. Loving requires more, needs grace more, calls forth more, echoes the first and great commandment more nearly and more deeply, than does respecting. Yet that implication is there, rich in consequence, relevant.

The ellipsis must be interpreted. If one fills it out, "You should love your neighbor as you happen to love yourself," many a manner of mischief may ensue. What if a person hates himself? Is he to hate his neighbor? The context of Matthew and the gospels should make it clear that it is not a precept to trust one's heart, as it is and as it storms, for the standard of respect and caring. I suggest that the ellipsis may be expanded: you should love your neighbor as you should love yourself — joyfully, faithfully, and in hope.

The Golden Rule is not an injunction for masochists to become sadists, to inflict on others the pain they wish for themselves. What would we be, when we would soundly be?

General principles imply or support subsidiary principles. The biblical formulations relate the Summary of the Law and the Golden Rule to the law and the prophetic word.

The immediate context of Leviticus to "Love thy neighbor as thyself " relates the precept to the first part of the Law and to subsidiary and consequent moral truths.

". . . Ye shall be holy: for I the Lord your God am holy." (19.2)

"Ye shall not steal, neither deal falsely, neither lie one to another." (19.11)

"Ye shall do no unrighteousness in judgment: thou shalt not respect the person of the poor, nor honour the person of the mighty . . ."(19.15)

"Thou shalt not go up and down as a talebearer among thy people . . ." (19.16)

"Thou shalt not hate thy brother in thine heart: thou shalt in any wise rebuke thy neighbour, and not suffer sin upon him." (19.17)

"Thou shalt not avenge, nor bear any grudge against the children of thy people, but thou shalt love thy neighbor as thyself: I am the Lord." (19.18)

"Ye shall do no unrighteousness in judgment . . ., in weight or in measure." (19.35)

"Just balances, just weights, a just ephah, and a just hin, shall ye have: I am the Lord your God, which brought you out of the land of Egypt." (19.36)

Stealing, dealing falsely, lying, being partial at law, hating, gossiping, avenging, bearing grudges — each of these is not loving, and consequently forbidden. The proscription of each is (1) a precept (2) a precept clearly standing under a more general precept, (3) a precept of very wide application (whether absolutely unexceptionable or not). The "just hin" and "just ephah" — fair measuring, a very important moral concept — follow both from the love of neighbor and the love of truth.

One precept, reproving one's neighbor, certainly seems less widely applicable. If one loves himself with any soundness, he certainly shall reprove himself when he does something shameful, something that spots his life and may well damage his flourishing (self-prudence is a virtue). Therefore, if he cares for his neighbor, and his neighbor is doing something shameful, why should not the rule apply, and why should it not be a universal requirement to reprove every neighbor one thinks is doing something shameful?

The Golden Rule at that point seems to lead to a conflict with the corollary from the precept of loving neighbors, since we certainly don't want, even on our sounder days, for every person who knows us to reprove us each time that person thinks we are doing something wrong. Please, thank you not.

The issue is complicated, and several principles of some importance are involved, including others that flow from the precept of Love (respecting privacy, for one) or the excellent counsel in Proverbs 11.12, "... a man of understanding holdeth his peace."

Here as elsewhere, when principles conflict or apparently conflict, distinctions can be helpful. Proverbs 9.8 nicely fits (though, in rebuking even a wise man, some caution of tone is advised): "Reprove not a scorner, lest he hate thee: rebuke a wise man, and he will love thee."

That is, one should always love; one should sometimes, in some contexts and by some considerations, reprove.

Consequently, the proposition 'every moral or aesthetic principle is universal in form and admits no exceptions' is false. Milder and more defensible is the proposition 'Some moral and aesthetic principles are universal in form and admit no exceptions'.

Such principles are hard to come by. Many strong and widely applicable principles admit to at least a few exceptions, and principles stand in complex relation to other principles (as possibly conflicting, as fundamental or derived, and so on) and in complex relation to judgment, since we use principles, we develop conceptual and extra-conceptual skills in handling them, and do not merely reach aesthetic and moral conclusions by straightforward inferences. (The "merely" is also important since some judgment is straightforward, for instance: such-and-such an act would be shameful; therefore, do not do it.)

The Golden Rule and the second half of the Summary of the Law, are very general in application, obligatory as Law for Christians and Jews, can be supported by arguments (the previous chapter offered some for "treat people as people," a version or corollary of "Love thy neighbor"), and widely believed and supported by people who are neither Christians nor Jews. These two closely related precepts qualify very well as Law.

NATURAL LAW

Are these precepts natural laws? That depends, on some things and some meanings. While moral and universal in intent, the laws are not universal in form, and rigging them as such makes for awkwardness, unnaturalness, and probable misrepresentation. The proposition 'Every act which one does toward a neighbor should be loving and motivated by such love as one should manifest towards one's self' is fairly accurate but narrower than the precept 'love thy neighbor as thyself ' since love is not merely actions. "One should always love one's neighbor as oneself," the simplest translation from imperative to indicative, is not, strictly, in universal form. The form 'Every person should love every other person as he loves himself' is ambiguous in the reference of "he" and "himself," an awkward ambiguity to cure, and the problem could be exacerbated by insisting on 'he or she', 'himself or herself'. (The pronoun *he* is sometimes generic, sometimes masculine, and no easy resolution is in sight.) The notion of universality itself, then, requires some explaining.

Do the precepts of the Golden Rule and The Summary of the Law meet Thomas Hobbes's requirement for the Law of Nature, that it be "agreeable to the reason of all men"?[8] Observably not, since very many people do not believe in any natural law and hence do not believe in these precepts as natural law. One can reply, in Hobbes's words, "The unwritten law of nature, though it be easy to such, as without partiality, and passion, make use of their natural reason, and therefore leaves the violaters thereof without excuse; yet considering there be very few, perhaps none, that in some cases are not blinded by self love, or some other passion, it is now become of all laws the most obscure; and has consequently the greatest need of able interpreters."[9]

That may well be, but is *ad hominem* against disagreers, and logically cancels the appeal to *actual* universal testimony.

Nor are the precepts natural law in the sense that they are offered as based on reasoning. They simply are not. In Old Testament and New Testament they are offered on religious authority, which has proven, to the distress of rationalism, a firmer historical and personal base for morality than philosophical reasoning.

The Christian traditional position is that certain precepts of law which are known by revelation can also be proven by natural reasoning, when it is clear of prejudice and the heart's confusions. Hence one can never say that they are established by mere reason, since, first, reason alone cannot cure the heart so that the reason can reason truly; and, even if it could, it would still not be 'reason alone', since reason is not alone; it is create, a reflection and echo of Divine Reason.

LYING

When are universal principles sufficient? And which principles are universal? More important, how is one to use principles for judgment? To explore such issues, let us look next at the example of lying.

Take two statements. 'Lying is frequently morally wrong'. 'Lying is always wrong'. Every morally competent person (at least when not carrying philosophical banners) would agree without argument that the first statement is true. One has to judge to which instances of lying the statement applies, but it is a widely accepted, valuable guide to action. The second statement would provoke more disagreement. Some would deny it, on the ground that lying may sometimes be a moral duty (say, in wartime under certain conditions, or to protect the innocent, or to avoid giving social offense); others would affirm that lying is intrinsically wrong and hence is wrong on any occasion. But neither group would, one hopes, be quite happy with the position adopted. To call lying a duty, even sometimes, is sufficiently discomforting; and those that take the stronger line should at least be bothered by degrees and kinds of lying, borderline instances, and occasions when the precept not to lie seems to conflict with other duties or precepts.

To take a traditional sort of example, suppose a would-be murderer is pursuing an innocent victim, asks where the victim has gone, and will believe what you say.[10] Suppose further that you know where the pursued one is, that if you tell the truth the victim will be killed, that if you lie the victim will escape, that nothing else bad will be a consequence (and suppose anything else necessary to make the example pure): lying will lead to a good consequence, not-lying to a bad consequence. Should you lie to the potential murderer?

One response is to refuse to play the game. The example is hypothetical, and seldom if ever in real life is a lie *that* much called for. The consequences are distinctly hypothetical, since we never know or can know the full consequences of any action. That in itself is one good argument against going against a strong moral concept simply on a judgment of consequences. But consequences are nonetheless relevant to judgment; the virtue of prudence certainly includes paying some mind to reasonably foreseeable consequences; and one of the strongest arguments against lying is that lying destroys trust, an argument concerning consequences.

One could half play the game, accept some but not all of the supposing. For instance, in an actual situation where a murderer was pursuing a person whose whereabouts you knew, there would be other options than lying or truth-telling. One could keep silent, a courageous alternative. One could equivocate, at least a lesser ill than full-fledged lying. One could evade the question, variously stall for time, attack the potential murderer, or adopt other options. One could tell the truth and then phone the cavalry or the Canadian Mounted Police, having them arrive exactly in the nick of time to save the victim from harm. Dangerous? Not at all, since the arrival in time would be exactly as guaranteed as anything else in the hypothesis, that is, perfectly guaranteed, by the hypothesis.

One could make the false statement boldly; and later argue, with some plausibility, that it was not lying, since the villain had so far violated the bonds of society as not to be entitled to truth. That, however, is a dangerous move in a fallen world, since such reasoning could be used in support of many a wrongdoing.

It is relevant that soldiers under the gravest of duress are not required to lie, but to give only their name, rank, and number, and keep silence. Heroic virtue is required of actual human beings.

But suppose the occasion does arise, as in the hypothesis, or actually in life, when lying is morally needful, what then? We still need to distinguish. On such occasions, one should do what need be done, but at least with some reserve of private grimness, of strong doubt whether (in most instances) greater prior virtue or greater achieved wisdom might not have avoided the occasion of the lie.

There are degrees of lying, from the white lie on social occasions (not wholly non-culpable, since usually avoidable with a little tact and humor, and tending at least to weaken taste and communication) to grave lies always to be avoided, in Peter Geach's words, "lies that gravely injure our neighbor, including those that corrupt his understanding . . . apostasy from the Faith."[11]

Lying is, intrinsically and logically, a great evil. To-say-the-thing-which-is-not[12] insults God, the Author of being, the Truth of truth. It violates the very nature of the mind. It corrupts trust and thereby mars the fabric of human society. The truth that lying is widespread in human society and in the human soul is hard evidence for the reality of Original Sin.

Lying then, as such, is intrinsically and inherently wrong. It is wrong to speak as true what one knows is not true. It is wrong to speak any untruth, because one should conform one's mind to truth. It is very wrong to speak untruth knowingly for to speak so is to be untrue. All lies are false; so be true.

Those arguments are not tautologous, but they approach. Truth and troth are deeply interposed.

What is intrinsically wrong is always, in some real and deep sense, wrong. Hence the proscription of lying is, in a real and deep sense, universal. Lying is always wrong as an ingredient of an act, and actual occasions where one has a moral need to assert-as-truth falsehood knowingly are, for most professions, very rare. The proposition 'lying is sometimes morally good' not only sounds inconsistent, it *is* inconsistent; hence the generalization does and should remain general.

The moral example parallels aesthetic ones. For instance, unconsciously awkward language is always, in itself, an aesthetic flaw in a literary work, but does not automatically make the work in question a poor one. Virtually every work is guilty of some inept phrasing, and some important works may have a good deal of it. Still it is a flaw whenever it occurs, and unless a work is extraordinary in other ways, a large amount is fatal.

UNIVERSAL PRINCIPLES

One kind of universal principle appears in such statements as "Murder is always wrong" and "Literary impropriety is always wrong." Both statements are true and *partially* true by definition. Self-defence is not really murder; mock-epic is not really improper. Every murder is wrong because murder has come to mean only those examples of homicide which are morally (or legally) wrong. Literary impropriety implies wrong (i.e., improper) relations between subject and style, etc. The statements are true and, in a frustrating way, universal, as they have built into them, hidden in them, a means of rejecting exceptions. But, though they are in some respect tautologous, they also have real meaning. The assertion that murder is always wrong includes the very important notion that some examples of homicide are morally wrong. The statement about literary impropriety includes the notion that proper or improper relations can obtain between work and subject and style and author and audience, one of the most central of literary ideas. Generalizations such as these are principles involving value and in a real sense universal.

The demand placed on universals has been too great, and the consequent rejection of them is more thorough than need be. Swellings much resemble hollows. But principles of moral and literary judgment do exist; they are patently valuable; and some of them are universal in form (or can be made universal in form by rephrasing), however metaphysically potent or overrated that form may be. "Every" is not magic, nor does thinking just deal with or from "every." Many aesthetic statements beginning with "Every" are false ("Every protagonist should be named Henry"); but one can, by the right sort of qualifying or, if you will, finagling, produce an indefinite number of true ones. Some follow. The low voltage is deliberate.

Every good novel should show some skill in the handling of plot or character or theme.

Every good lyric poem should express feeling.

Every good political novel is something more than crudely melodramatic propaganda.

Every good traditional epic is longer than ten verses.

Every one of the best seventeenth-century metaphysical lyrics is ingenious and expressive.

Every good comic short story should be funny.

Every section of *Gulliver's Travels* has considerable literary merit.

Every good literary work should delight or instruct, or both.

Every good serious epic has a serious style.

One could obviously go on indefinitely. None of the statements are richly exciting or sufficient to turn ordinary men into infallible critics, but they do share some features:

(1) they are all true; (2) they are virtually undebatable; (3) none of them is merely tautologous, though some come closer than others; (4) all involve both aesthetic judgment and matter of 'fact'; (5) all of them are universal in form. That is, they are general literary principles which admit of no exceptions, and hence, however timid they may appear, constitute a proof that such propositions exist.

They are in one way not completely general. They do not apply to all works of literature without exception. To ask that of a principle is to ask a great deal. Yet there are principles that meet even that test:

No good work of literature is consistently boring to all good readers.

Every good literary work shows some power of expression and achieves some formal order.

Every good literary work expresses some proper attitudes.

Every good literary work implies or suggests some important truths about human experience.

Every good literary work is in some sense a representation of life.

Every good literary work is in some degree an expression of the authors' individuality.

Every good literary work is, so to speak, a just and lively image of reality.

These principles are not new or surprising, and do not take us very far toward sound literary judgment, though they have value. But they are universal, evaluative, informative, and true, and they do apply to every work of literary art without exception, even to bad and indifferent ones by implication.

JUDGMENT

Here are some statements not entirely singular or entirely universal, statements about literature which I consider valuable and true. Some are debatable. Some are not very debatable. Some are cribbed. Some would rather naturally be called principles; to some we would deny that name or would hesitate to assign it. At least they will raise the question whether we have a very clear idea of what we mean by, or expect from, literary principles. We should not mean or expect too much, or too little.

Samuel Richardson tends to be too gushy, Jane Austen too cool, though both are admirable novelists.

William Carlos Williams's theories about poetry are confused, valuable in helping us understand his own excellent poetry; and an encouragement to laxity of style and rhythm in some of his followers.

Many modern poets are too self-effacingly and self-ironically cute.

Certain comic works, notably Ben Jonson's *Volpone* and William Faulkner's "Spotted Horses," reach a depth of metaphysical horror in portraying the perversions and confusions in human justice.

The will cannot do the work of the imagination; but neither can the imagination do the work of the will.

Art perfects nature.

Sometimes artistry of style becomes too visible.

The chief temptation of free verse is to slide into medley, or prose.

Jonathan Swift is a master of plain style, Sir Thomas Browne of highly figured style.

Laurence Sterne's *Tristram Shandy* is imperfectly ordered, but in many ways brilliantly ordered, and for all its good fun and sentimental benevolence is at times so morally perceptive as to be terrifying.

The list can go on and on and on. Such statements are literary criticism; they are not universal in form; they do not apply themselves; they are neither infallible nor capricious; they do help us compare and judge; they are reached neither by simple intuition nor pure reasoning; to understand them or apply them one must be able to respond to, and to think about, literature. They stand or fall as judgment. Informed and responsible and imaginative judgment is, in varying degrees, possible.

But one cannot toss theory aside, or pitch all weight on the particular case. In each of the above statements, the particular, singular, and general fit each other in ways more complex than one is apt to pound into nice logical paradigms. Judgment is prior to epistemological pigeonholes. We need to think about singulars, even though we never exhaust them by thinking about them. Good judgment needs good theory, at least implicitly. Theory can strengthen literary

understanding; it can lead away from or distort literary understanding
when it sets up as a separate kingdom or as the final cause of literature.
The relations between theory and judgment are dense and individual.
Perhaps the most fundamental relation is that good judgment uses
theory; it is not theory's creature or theory's servant. One corollary
of high rank is that good criticism should lean heavily on particular
criticism. Principles should be tested against poems, poems against
principles.

Here an opponent (a, let me hope, stronger-than-straw man) may
say, "Ah! By making judgment prior to theory, you maintain an
antitheoretical theory and such theories are inevitably self-inconsistent."
Perhaps; but I am not persuaded. A theory which maintains the
fundamental invalidity of theory undercuts itself, but to claim that
theory is a valid but limited instrument is not, so far as I can see, self-
inconsistent.

That theory is itself true, and limited. It will not take the place of
judgment in judging literary works. It is arrived at by judgment.

But judgment, it may be urged, must have some basis, and that basis
must be solid theoretical principle. That argument is impressive, but
not, finally, satisfactory. For "basis" is a metaphor, albeit a good one,
and in some ways crucially misrepresents the issues. Why should
principles "stand under" aesthetic and moral discussions? Those
discussions are not parrots on perches. Further, a defense of even a
fairly strict rationalism is self-inconsistent if it has nothing stronger to
offer than a metaphorical argument. Metaphors are not demonstrative;
they are useful and must be used with good judgment.

But, comes the obvious retort, if a judgment isn't soundly based on
good theory, it is arbitrary and capricious, and literary discussion must
cease to make any sense. If one refutes the rationalist, one is left with
silence. Again, not so. The disjunction is false, a variant or neighbor
of the nation that we must have either absolute rational certainty (or
very high and verifiable probability) or a scepticism in which all moves
lead equally nowhere. There just is — and we all experience it — a
middle ground. Good literary judgement is not simply an inference
from clear principles, nor merely a heaping-up of 'fact', nor an
undiscussable intuition. There is something informed and thoughtful,
and something undiscussable, about it, and the epistemology which
will corral and tame the relations is not yet to be had.

Or we can say (after all, the metaphor "basis" is a powerful and natural one) that of course good literary judgment is soundly based, but that the basis is not merely or even necessarily abstract theory. Good literary judgment is "based" on feeling, thought, experience, comparison, inference, listening, information, responding, analyzing, good luck, hard work. Why single out one of the real bases as somehow the only real one? As Wittgenstein beautifully says, "these foundation walls are carried by the whole house."[13]

But surely, the plausible moan returns, we can't validly believe what we don't have good reason to believe, and that sends us back to principle. The premise is true to the edge of tautology, the conclusion false. For a reason, even a very good reason, need not be a principle. A man goes to market to buy a pig. The pig is the reason, but hardly a principle. There are lots of good reasons for doing and believing. These reasons do imply or suggest principles (not necessarily universal ones), but the reasons are not simply principles and it is not an act of principled inference which brings reasons and principles and singulars to coordination. What does that, then, if it is done? Judgment.

Or, to put it another way, a good cabinet-maker needs good tools. He makes the cabinet with the tools. He does not ask the tools which one to use at what time. *He* uses the tools. How did he learn to use the tools? By being told some truths, by getting the "feel" of the operations, by practicing. The tools are in the analogy the literary principles and reasons. My analogy is of course just an analogy, but it has one powerful advantage over the "basis" metaphor. Literary judgment, like cabinet making, is a human activity. To analyze the active purely in terms of the passive or static is precisely to deny what is active. (Several important and invalid arguments for determinism depend on just such a confusion.)

Or, if the cabinet metaphor seems too ordinary, there is the organic metaphor, a much-lauded metaphor and of course a valuable one. A flower garden requires good soil and good seed and good knowledge and good skill. Beauty requires the mysterious and the known. One cannot raise flowers, without soil or seed, by rational fiat. The artifact and organic metaphors are both great and traditional metaphors. So is the metaphor of the base. But no such metaphors apply themselves. That requires judgment.

THE LIMITS OF ANALYSIS

Judgments about singulars are apt to be firmer (better based, as it were) than the reasons and analyses adduced to support them. There is more disagreement over whether the *Iliad* is a well-unified poem than over whether it is a great poem. Our trained response is apt to be more, not less, precise than our analyzing. We often analyze to show what we have already, before the analysis, seen. The following couplet of Pope's is brilliant and discussable: "Yes, I am proud; I must be proud to see/Men not afraid of God, afraid of me."[14] It can be discussed biographically (Pope's cunning and moral verve collide, and sustain each other), or rhetorically (the parallel of "God" and "me" is impudent and sharp), or metrically ("proud" and "proud" receive like stressing; so do "afraid" and "afraid"; the pairing of the two pairs, with their dance of relationships, is somewhere near the heart — or heartlessness — of his meaning). The analysis is, at least I mean it to be, true; but it is other than and necessarily less than the couplet. In reading the couplet one experiences the reality of the couplet in its meaning and its quality. In talking about it, we can point out and point up, but we cannot render. Analysis of verse is by nature partial; the verses are their own event. I belabor a commonplace; it is a true commonplace which sets a limit beyond which theory and analysis in real senses cannot pass, and should not try to pass.

Insofar as analysis is, as its name suggests, a breaking-down into parts, it is self-inconsistent as well as observably false to talk about exhaustive analysis. For a survey of the parts of an object, even if that survey, *per impossibile*, could cover every single part and all the mutual relations of the parts, would still be a multiplicity, not a whole. Or if one wishes to say that the survey is a whole, the summing-up of all the parts, that whole is a different whole from the object. Wholes and parts have paradoxical relationships which analyzers and theorists had better respect, even if it takes some tempering of zeal. *We don't, after all, know very much.* Further it is plainly true that no analysis does in fact cover all the parts and relationships within an object. Cowboys know some things about cows that zoologists don't, zoologists some things that cowboys don't and they should respect each others' knowledge and ignorance. If my analogy tends to class literary critics with veterinarians, neither cowboys nor zoologists but a bit of both, the veterinarians I know are courteous and will not mind.

I beg indulgence for one more, queerish analogy. Literary analysis is not picking up lumps out of a box; nor is it pointing to the pedestal (basis) a poem sits on; nor is it even cutting where the joints are. It is more like using an X-ray machine. What we see (1) is elsewhere; (2) is miscolored; (3) is misshapen; (4) needs interpretation; (5) gives clues to but does not change the reality of the object examined (with the fascinating exception — let the theorist heed — that if one is X-rayed too often, one dies); (6) is, properly understood, true; and (7) can be very important in understanding the object. Most of all, an X-ray machine needs a skilled interpreter, with good eyes and strong and practiced judgment. Human activity is what we do.

SUMMARY

This chapter maintains the following statements.

(1) Value-realism is implied by the assertion that principles admit exceptions.

(2) Judgment does not consist merely of applying principles to individual instances.

(3) Many useful moral and aesthetic principles admit exceptions.

(4) Good judgment consists (in part) of balancing claims and conflicts of principles.

(5) Some principles are more fundamental than others and hence are helpful in choosing between others when there is conflict.

(6) Some moral precepts are very basic, namely the Golden Rule and the Summary of the Law (the non-Christian reader will likely prefer to concentrate on the second part of the Summary, "love thy neighbor as thyself," but it would have been fair to neither my convictions nor the argument to have omitted the Christian context.)

(7) Those basic precepts are widely accepted, and can be strongly supported by argument. They are, to Christian and Jew, Law, and worth the serious attention and reflection of others, as Law.

(8) Those precepts immediately imply and support some other precepts, such as being holy, not stealing, not gossiping, not lying, not bearing grudges, being righteous in judgment, precepts which, whether universal or not ("being righteous in judgment" is totally universal), important and widespread principles admitting few exceptions at most.

(9) Whether such Law is natural law depends on some distinctions

and definitions concerning (among other things) universality of form, unwrittenness, and being supported or established by reason. It is concluded that these Laws are natural law and that this book consequently supports natural law, but that God's Law as God's Law is more basic and historically more supporting of morality, than God's Law as natural law.

(10) The issue of universality in relation to some precepts, for instance, lying and certain aesthetic precepts, is complex, that some principles (including the proscription of lying) are in genuine senses universal, and that the demand on universals has often been too great. Rules matter and cannot be tossed aside casually, or situationally, but do not suffice as judgment.

(11) The relations between theory and judgment are dense and individual.

(12) Principles should be tested against actual literary works and actual moral situations, and literary works and moral situations should be tested against principles.

(13) "Basis" is (1) sometimes a useful metaphor but (2) only a metaphor.

(14) Literary and moral judgements are human activities, requiring tools, knowledge, and experience.

(15) Analysis is valuable, limited, a dangerous master, a useful servant, a sometimes pleasant and sometimes relevant game.

(16) Judgment is possible, and neither infallible nor capricious. We are we, in the peril of human judgment.

5

The Magic Word Culture

'Cultures differ'. Yes, and no, and so? And some other things.

That little assertion 'Cultures differ' has done much moral and philosophical damage in our century, and usually by a vague kind of misdirecting. It is magically uttered, in a special tone of voice; and some vaguely-conceived conclusions are supposed to follow so evidently as to be immune to analysis or argument. A favorite conclusion is 'It's all a matter of opinion', usually if ludicrously combined with 'Everyone has a right to his own opinion'. If 'Everyone has a right to his own opinion', there is at least one right, value-realism is consequently true, and one major intended meaning of the muddled 'It's all a matter of opinion' is false. 'It's all a matter of opinion' combines in a drifty mist of non-thought, several opinions: that people sometimes disagree about moral and aesthetic issues (which is true), that there is no ground whatever to any opinion in such matters, that absolutely no evidence is available including that being offered in the argument (which is mainly false, but also self-inconsistent), that in moral and aesthetic issues every opinion is equally true and hence worthy of respect (which is false, self-inconsistent and inconsistent with the previous meaning), and so on. Without more ado, I'll let the sentence 'It's all a matter of opinion' go on its rattle-brained and unstoppable way.

Another frequent inference from the statement 'Cultures differ' is the virtue of tolerance. 'What right', it is frequently and firmly asserted in these or similar words, 'does one have to make moral judgments of other people and other cultures?' The word *right* entails value-realism and itself makes a cross-cultural judgment, namely, that no one in any culture has a right to make cross-cultural judgments. Such a question normally presumes that one may and should make judgments of approval of other cultures, but not judgments of disapproval. A

55

scramble of inconsistency, especially if used, as frequently, to oppose natural law concepts, since a natural-law concept is implied. Yet there are truths in or hovering near that sort of ill-formed question: one should treat people as people, with basic courtesy; one should judge in context and on relevant evidence; one should not dismiss the unfamiliar because it is unfamiliar when conflicts of moral concepts occur; one should reflect before deciding. However, one should not decide in advance that, after reflection, one will decide that the conflicting moral concepts are equally true, which would be twice-inconsistent: one would not actually be thinking (having already decided) and, if the concepts actually conflict, they cannot both be true. What one may decide, sometimes, is that apparent conflicts are not real, that a divergence between two cultures may come from, not a disagreement in basic concept, but in a difference of circumstance in which the basic concepts are applied.

Myriad confusions exist, but one need not unwind them one by one. Any cross-cultural thinking that prohibits cross-cultural thinking is, at root, unsound.

One need not go to the Trobriand Islands to find out that human beings disagree. Families differ; juries differ; human controversy and contention is no news. The dissidence of dissent in human affairs is loud, long, and not very encouraging; it is a false logical move for a controversialist to argue that controversial positions are inherently inarguable because controversial. Or inherently equal.

Different nations and societies have differences in moral belief and similarity in moral belief, real divergences and impressive overlap and accord. Unanimity of moral opinion would not prove the opinions true, and divergences prove nothing automatically. If human beings are moral creatures capable of error, sin, and confusion, divergence and overlap should be expected.

Judgment in relation to situations and contexts often lessens apparent divergences. Most modern Americans do not have a duty to learn camelmanship, or even horsemanship; many modern Americans do have a duty, an important one, to learn automobileship. Some general precepts fit all three moral skills: control thoughtfully; learn relevant truths; practice; do not overestimate your skill; exercise the right mix of prudence and courage (timid drivers are hazards); respect other travellers.[1] Some precepts and conditions do not fit all three: automobiles are not sentient or especially fond of oats.

We can learn from other societies; that is a good truth and good hope. When there are differences, one needs to ask what and why, to determine relevant differences, to see what apparent differences vanish or lessen because of distinctions or circumstances, to see what precepts are fundamental, to do whatever one needs to do to discriminate and imagine and understand. Insofar as the differences do not resolve, one must judge what is right, insofar as such judgment is relevant to our real living and thinking. We do not each have to decide everything!

Of the many, many thousands of possible examples of likenesses and divergences between precepts of societies, civilizations, and tribes, I shall take one, in order to exemplify structural and logical possibilities and some basic moves. The concern will be between fairly normal and typical modern moral thinking and some Babylonian precepts.

Sections 53 & 54 of the *Code of Hammurabi* follow:

"If a man have neglected to strengthen his dike, and have not strengthened it, and a break have been made in his dike, and the water carry away the meadow, the man in whose dike the break has been made shall restore the grain which he has caused to be lost.

"If he be not able to restore the grain, they shall sell him and his goods for money, and the people of the meadow whose grain was carried away shall share it.[2]

My concern is not any legal point, but whether the law is morally right, just, fair. Hammurabi claims that his laws are just: "I put justice and righteousness into the language of the land, and promoted the welfare of the people."[3] He was not a legal positivist.

We (that is, some fairly normal and typical modern moral thinking) would agree, at least in principle, with #53 and disagree with #54. The principle of agreement might be stated: 'A man is responsible for damage caused by his neglect to maintain property or equipment for which he is clearly responsible'. It's hard to imagine any society which would not accept the principle or to imagine any society which would not have a problem in deciding degree (of neglect or of liability) and in deciding what circumstances may mitigate, in particular cases. The principle stands under the principle, 'A man is responsible to do his legitimate tasks well, with consideration for other people', a moral precept (natural law) which is (or very near to being) without exception. The 'legitimate' is meant to exclude two kinds of case, examples of which are doing sabotage in Vichy France (which the worker might consider his dangerous duty), and being in a coma. People in comas do not (then, and as such) have legitimate tasks.

The more specific principle is itself universal or near universal, and universal also are the difficulties of interpretation, with respect to degree, and to applying to actual instances.

We would reject #54, since our society does not approve of slavery and allows pleas of bankruptcy. The divergences are blunt; what are the moves for dealing with such divergences?

First, we can ignore them. After all, we do not live in ancient Babylon, and it is not part of our duty to decide what was or was not just in their laws. That is a sensible move, and naturally enough, what we normally do. And it has logical validity: we do not have to decide about topics we do not have to decide about, a moral truth of consequence. I can hardly take that escape route, however, since I offered the example. Deciding has logical relevance to the questions at hand.

Second, we can say that we are right and they were wrong about both issues (slavery and bankruptcy). On slavery, most (all?) modern relativists would fervently take the anti-slavery side; they do not think that slavery is an issue to be treated just as a matter of opinion or cultural preference. People do disagree about that issue; issues do not always get peaceably resolved. The American Civil War happened.

Bankruptcy is a milder issue and admits more degrees. One can think that bankruptcy law is at times too lenient without wishing to disallow all bankruptcy. One can believe that bankruptcy law is at times too harsh without supporting bankruptcy on instant demand.

Third, we can say that #54 was right for the Babylonians, but not for us. The idiom 'right for' and 'true for' deserve a closer look, since the idioms have some good senses, some confused senses, and some non-senses. It's 'true for' me, and no other human being, that there is visible, this minute, to me a particular copy of a picture of a Pterosaur skeleton and silhouette in overlapping design, and a specific, actual Norway Spruce cone (both are beautiful), and it is also true that no other human being currently can see those two objects. But even that statement is misleading. Those objects are in this room now (at the writing of the first draft) and are visible to me — that truth is true and hence a truth for everybody whether they know about it or not. Further, if given the proper space-time references, that proposition will be permanent truth, including the beauty.

'Ah', a facticist may interrupt, 'the presence of the Norway Spruce cone is a fact; the beauty is merely your subjective judgment'. Flatly, no. Anyone thinking that Norway Spruces aren't beautiful is aesthetically incompetent, and there's an end on it. Or, put a little more politely, there is widespread agreement on the beauty of Norway Spruces. A highly competent professional writes, "Norway Spruce has been widely cultivated for ornament, shade, shelterbelts, Christmas trees, and forest plantations. The showy cones are the largest of the spruces."[4] I am quite sure (probability of 1.0) that the cone and the tree I found it under are beautiful; I am only virtually sure (say, 0.98) that it is a Norway Spruce. The identification was positive, but my tree identifications have been mistaken in the past, and not all similar varieties with different names are given in manuals.

Any truth 'for' a person of something individual (location, actual physical perspective, memory, or other) becomes public truth as soon as it is well stated.

The idioms 'right for' and 'true for' can mean fitting one's experience, or character, or person. 'True for me' can mean true in one's experience, the repetitively autobiographical; or when a shoe salesman says, 'That's right for you', he means both fit (hence comfort) and style. The judgment about comfort (a judgment of value) is readily falsifiable. Pain speaks truth. When a tailor says, 'That's right for you', the judgment is professional and complex, involving physiology, character, color, and other factors. He does not mean primarily that the customer will like the clothing, but that the clothing fits well and is proper for the wearer, and that competent judges will agree.

The uses, so far, are fairly innocent but can mislead. Other uses are more troublesome. The idiom 'true for'[5] a person, when it means believed to be true by that person, always is an ill-formed expression, since the idiom makes truth and falsity logically compatible. It was 'true for' Lucretius that heavier objects necessarily fall proportionally faster than lighter objects, but it is not true that heavier objects necessarily fall proportionally faster than lighter objects.[6]

The idiom 'true for' can be an ill-formed expression meaning true under certain circumstances. It is ill-formed because it allows truth and falsity to sound compatible, and because the statement fails to say what it means. The statement 'It was true for the ancient Babylonians that slavery was morally right' can mean at least two quite different things: (1) the ancient Babylonians believed slavery to be morally right, and (2) under the circumstances in ancient Babylon, slavery was morally right.

The idiom 'true for' often unfocuses, by an overlap-and-dissolve, the various meanings discussed and is apt in the bad bargain to include also obscure and vague, partially or illusorily-grasped, would-be meaning. The term is systematically and unsystematically misleading and distorting. It should be avoided, or given the relevant qualifications to make its intended sense clear, in any specific use.

Where circumstances make differences, apparent differences can vanish. If there was something peculiar about the circumstances that made slavery right in Babylon, then there is no incompatibility of the institutions. But on this issue, most modern (non-communistic) thinkers do not believe that there are circumstances sufficiently compelling to make slavery a widespread and acceptable institution.

Laws of different countries are never, as such, logically incompatible, since Hammurabi was not telling Americans that we had better watch our dikes, and Lincoln was not emancipating Babylonians. It is the very considerable overlap and agreement among moral beliefs of different nations and societies and our drive for universalism that occasions reflection on likenesses and differences. It really goes against a deep grain to think there is no moral truth or that, except when peculiar circumstances intervene, moral truth is not universal. One of the deepest strands of agreement is simply the belief in moral truth itself. Societies have divergent beliefs about morality; they almost universally, until very modern times, believed that people really were behaving badly when they violated morality. The cultures offered in evidence for relativism are or were not themselves relativistic.

Within this specific comparison to the Babylonian code, other moves are possible. One could cite moral progress (a bold belief in the 1980s), but that, too, is to say that slavery is wrong and that it took a while for people to realize that slavery is wrong. To say that slavery was not wrong then, but has become wrong, because of moral progress, in comparatively modern times, is inconsistent with the notion of moral progress itself. Change can be progress only if there is some standard which does not itself change; otherwise, the basis of comparison collapses (unless, perchance, one opted to fault the Babylonians for not *predictively* condemning American slavery). Progressivism and relativism — though often close companions — are, at logical root and branch, wholly incompatible.

One can adjudicate, with 'something to be said for both sides', faulting Hammurabi on slavery but finding in #54 at least some validity of principle suggesting that our bankruptcy practices are over-lenient.

In discussing apparent moral differences, we can choose between the divergent views, qualify by circumstances or by analysis, show that the apparent differences are not real differences. But those moves, or others, are *moves*: moral thinking. They do not, ever, reduce moral or aesthetic difference or likeness to indifference.

Men are fallible, active, deciding; they obey and disobey rules; they have views why they do things. If rocks have such views they are blessedly silent about it. Men also are moral beings. If a man does not believe rules to be genuinely right, one may get him to obey the rules as convenient, rational, or the like (therefore in some sense *right* — another complication), but it is surely irrational of him not to break any rules when he judges it to be to his own convenience to break them, unless he really believes he owes a duty to other people. The dilemma may be fudged or clouded in various ways, but can only be solved by a belief in the reality and intelligibility of value.

Relativism is a thicket in a marsh. Men do not follow different systems of rules; they hold and act on different (and greatly overlapping) moral beliefs. If all the beliefs are false, they are all false. If some are true and others contradict them, the latter are false. If some beliefs are true for certain circumstances, then they don't conflict with beliefs which are true for different circumstances, and there is no problem. And so on. Either value exists and is knowable, or not. The moral *anomie* (Durkheim's word is appropriate here)[7] of many young people is surely in real part a consequence of the academic and other teaching of relativism. A serious charge, seriously intended. Nor can one rationally use relativism to argue for tolerance. The relativist who is consistent should applaud the following boast: "Carnage suited me; heaven put these things/in me somehow. Each to his own pleasure!"[8]

(Relativism, being inconsistent in its foundations, cannot be consistent on all points, a truth of some polemical advantage to relativists.)[9]

If positivism is true, there is no aesthetic knowledge and consequently no literary criticism, dodge as we may. If relativism is true, all literary criticism is equally true, and hence equally false since it claims to discriminate. Often writers say that the critic's true job is to analyze, not evaluate, but that does not solve the problem since, on those grounds, analysis is of no value either. One could cheerfully turn the argument about and say that, since sometimes students certainly do learn to understand literature better, positivism and relativism are necessarily false, but that sort of confidence is rare enough to sound more like bravado rather than quiet certitude. But students do learn to understand literature better, and theories inconsistent with that truth are consequently proven to be false.

Every teacher of literature knows that some interpretations and criticisms are better than others and can give true reasons why. I once had a student who thought, until corrected, that Keats's "On First Looking into Chapman's Homer" was a baseball poem, about Chapman's four-base hit. If he was wrong, some interpretations are better than others, if some interpretations are *better* than others, then positivism in the narrow sense and relativism in many of its vapor-quick senses (that is, positivism and relativism in the damaging senses) are false. It is not probable, but certain, that he was wrong, and the readers of this book know that he was. Further, a criticism of the poem using that interpretation would be inferior *as* criticism to criticism which used the right interpretation of the title. Critical judgments of literature, then, can be right on certain evidence, evidence with a probability of one, even judgments a great deal more complex than my sample. The statement "Many of Shakespeare's sonnets display an extraordinary talent for rhythm and imagery" is true, certain, and quite complicated to arrive at.

Moral disagreement or aesthetic disagreement entails non-relativism. If two men disagree about a poem, one saying it is good, the other saying it is bad, the disagreement vanishes if it turns out that what their statements mean is merely that one is pleased by the poem and the other displeased, two perfectly consistent truths. But they surely think they are disagreeing; therefore they surely do not mean merely some psychological statement when they say "Poem *J* is bad"; "No; poem *J* is good."

But, the rejoinder rejoins, taste is dependent on "culture." We think Homer is good because we are part of our culture. A different culture, different standards. In such statements "culture" may be so general as to include everything except genetic structure. In that case its meaning includes everything, including valid value judgments if any, and hence cannot be used to reject value judgments or anything else. If the word does not have such a broad meaning, such statements are manifestly false. Homer's world is enormously different from ours, as well as much like ours. It is the likeness or the difference which determines the invalidity of the taste? Neither makes much sense, on serious reflection. Or such statements may mean that readers like Homer merely because they have been told to in advance, because it is a cultural belief imposed on them that Homer is a powerful poet. But many readers do respond powerfully to Homer, readers who do not always respond as they are told to.

But, it is further said, our responses depend on our nervous system. So our literary experiences and pleasures aren't "absolute," but relative to our experience. It is very hard to see what is meant by "absolute" in such a statement. Our experience is our experience, and in some senses (though not in every sense)[10] we know nothing apart from it. But that objection applies as strongly to other subjects, all other subjects, as to literary experience, and hence undercuts all positions with equal force (including relativism and positivism). If we can't fundamentally trust our experience, we are truly out of luck. All of us.

In some very important sense indeed, our knowledge stands on faith in experience. If that is so, then absolute rational certainty would seem impossible (except perhaps on a very few matters, and even then I have my doubts), for I do not see how one can prove the veracity of experience without assuming it. To attempt the proof, one has to assume the conclusion. Of course one has to assume the conclusion to carry on any argument; but necessity is not as such proof.[11] At the same time, arguments offered against that faith in experience tend to undercut themselves in a very special way; they have to assume the veracity of experience in order to cast doubt on it (this is one of several reasons why I believe that theism is more *rational* than opposing views). There is a middle ground between strict rationalism and strict scepticism

— namely, all of human experience and existence. It is a ground with limits and confusions and shadows, some of them dark. But we can and do stand on it, and we do and should make the act of faith it perpetually requires. That act of faith itself, and all the discussion we engage in depends on it, is non-relativistic and non-positivistic and non-sceptical. And relativists and positivists and sceptics *do* engage in the discussion.

6

Choosing Value

Since value is real, one is no more free to choose what one may correctly believe about value than one is free to choose what one may correctly believe about chemistry.

If value were not real, one would be mistaken in choosing to believe any value (or 'values') at all, since all such beliefs would be mistaken.

Or, put differently:

'Let's choose that all pine trees bear pears and haws. Let's choose that the Mississippi River is climbing the mountains of Spain. Let's choose that Robert Herrick had no metrical skill. Let's choose that it is all right for anyone who misdialed to be rude on the telephone to whoever answers. Let's choose that −2 is 7. Let's choose that examination papers may be justly graded at random. Let's choose a right to unlimited sexual freedom and to unlimited lying'.

Is such freedom grand?

7

Subject — Object

As soon as one calls a person a subject as over against objects, one has already falsified our experience, and troubles are begun.

The division seems to work grammatically, but does not. 'I see a tree' is grammatical, often true, and innocent-appearing. We analyze the sentence grammatically: "I" is the subject, "see" the verb, "a tree" the object. Therefore it seems to make sense to talk about the person as subject as over against the object, since the subject and object in the sentence are separated, hence somewhat 'over against' each other. But wait. 'A tree is seen by me'. Now "tree" is the subject, "is" a passive verb, "me" the object of a preposition. Grammar has reversed the subject-object relationship; and the observer (subject-become-object) has been kicked down a grammatical stair to a lower level.

In the sentence 'I see a tree', the subject and object are not over against each other. The subject is "I," the predicate "see the tree," and 'see' is not a linking verb to set things over against each other. Neither, strictly, are linking verbs mere links, setting subject and object over against each other. The following sentences have the linking verb *is*. 'Malcolm is my friend'. 'A raccoon is a mammal'. 'Four and three is seven'. 'The President of the United States is Commander-in-Chief of the Armed Forces'. The linking verb *is* has a different meaning in each sentence.

In the sentence 'I see a tree', "tree" is the object of "see," hence not the object of the subject. If one says, which makes sense, that 'a tree' takes the action of 'I see' ('see a tree' is an incomplete expression), then a verb obtrudes between subject and object.

The subject-object distinction does not stand grammatical analysis, whether or not it was partly occasioned by half-conscious grammatical

67

analysis to begin with (a historical question I cannot answer — that there was some influence of grammar seems very likely).

But, grammar or no, don't we look out on a world of objects? Well, our eyes see mostly forward and some peripherally, until we turn our heads. Then our eyes still see in front of most of the body. Nor is a world in front of us. The world is in front of us and in back of us, as we know though eyes look forth. Sometimes people are very much aware of that truth. Tales were told of sections of cities so tough that the patrolmen walked beats in pairs, back to back.

If subjects cloud knowledge insofar as they are subjects, then, since only subjects can have knowledge, all knowledge is as clouded as it is known. Then, wholly, a mist. But that is (clearly) not so.

Aesthetically, what is subject and object? Or are they? Where is beauty? Where is value? Or can one sensibly ask? In such statements as 'aesthetic value is in the object', "in" is a metaphor; and confusion flourishes when metaphors are leaned upon with more weight than they can bear. A beautiful waterfall is in space and is beautiful. It seems odd to say that its beauty is in space, odder yet to say that some part of the object is not in space. An odd dilemma. But to flee it by saying that the beauty is "in" the observer(s) is to flee to another and less clear metaphor. We divide the undivided to analyze, then use our analyses to deny the reality of the experience we had to assume to begin the analysis. A strange and comfortless procedure. In some senses beauty is "in" objects, waterfalls or poems; in other senses it makes only a confusing sort of meaning to call them "in" or "out." We stumble into some of the same puzzles with Berkeley or Kant, glaring at tables. Are the tables there or here? How do we know? Where and what is the seam between he who sees and what is seen?[1] We hesitate, and suspect that the trouble lies in the first step out of common experience into the special terms of the analysis. Secondary qualities, then primary qualities vanish before the philosophical glasses. We remove the glasses and the qualities move back in place. It should be the glasses we distrust, even if we cannot give an adequate analysis of the experience. Either we trust, within some reason, our experience or we don't; if we don't trust in the first place, we have no business to dismiss the experience by analyses that presume it. It is not, finally, "naive realism" that is naive. Judgment stands on and in our experience, and our experience has more than one thing to say.

First, there are senses in which value is 'in' the literary object. A dull reader misses beauties that are there; a more astute reader sees those beauties; a dull or astute reader is apt to misread and consequently have experiences of beauties or flaws not in the work. To deny that is to deny what is patently obvious in experience; it is also to deny the possibility of understanding or teaching literature. But if those statements are true, beauty is in objects.

Second, there is a plain and probably tautologous sense in which nothing whatever can be talked of "apart from" human perception and experience. If we talk of, we talk of. If we see, we see. But it remains true (and we all know it as firmly as we know anything) that trees exist in space when no human being is looking at them, and it remains true that the *Iliad* would be a great poem even if it had not survived. We wouldn't know of it or know that it is great, but it would nonetheless be great. It is certainly true that there have been good poems that no living human being knows of at present; some of them will be discovered in the future (manuscripts do show up, as they have in the past), many of them will not. The statement 'some poems are better than others' is not just an elaborate shorthand for an obscure something else. It is a statement about poems, just as much as 'the leaf is green' is a statement about a leaf, even though we cannot know leaves without experiencing them. That is, beauty is, in very real ways, in objects. More timidly, adjectives such as *beautiful* or *good* can be applied to literary work and do tell us something about the work itself, a very important something. In fact the most natural question to ask about a literary work (and probably the most frequently asked after "Who wrote it?") is "Is it good?"

But of course ordinary experience does not push us to the extremes of dichotomy either. Literary works are made by people for people; human response is deeply involved, as means to knowledge and as the final cause of the intent. In some sense every reading of a poem realizes, makes real, what existed as potentiality before. But if the poem is potentiality which is made real by human experiencing then its reality is defective until it is performed, experienced, felt. At the same time, many readings of a poem are imperfect — do not realize what is in the poem to realize or add what is not there. The work exists to be realized; it exists as a real entity that no experiencing quite perfectly catches; it is and is not 'in' minds. To the complex reality of literature and its experience, the analytical dichotomy of pure subject as against pure object simply does not do justice. Analysis strains what we know and can clearly say about individual poems. There is value in the poem and value in the experiencing, the values being neither equivalent nor independent. Most important, the truth of value-realism does not depend on the precise analysis of subject-object puzzles and confusions.

One sees a well-formed sugar maple in the autumn, red and orange and green and gold and very beautiful. Problem? None whatever: an event gladdening the heart with actual and known beauty.

'But beauty is in the eye of the beholder'. Well, yes, sort of. We see beauty. Also, by that reckoning, in the eye of the beholder are the sugar maple, the ground, the sky, the cats, the horses, the mountains and more. Is the eye crowded? Is it scratched by the cats in it? Thou hypocrite, first cast out the tree out of thine own eye. If the tree offend thee, pluck it out. And try again.

'Beauty is merely in the subjective judgment of the beholder. But the mountains are there, actual, physical facts, agreed on'. No! Most people, all aesthetically competent people, who see the Appalachian Mountains, agree that they are often beautiful, a question of value. No one can tell how many mountains and hills constitute the Appalachian Mountains, a question of 'fact'.

'I'm beginning to believe that you are serious about the fact-value business'. That's right. The distinctions won't do.

One can make a case that a scientific description of the events of perception unsticks the solid world we think we 'objectively' know, out there. Roughly, light waves go from a tree (whatever or non-ever that is) out there to our visual apparatus, eyes and nerves and brain (or mind? problems occur, whichever one says) and our brain from the data constitutes a world and projects it outward into space and simultaneously gives us the illusion that *that* is what we are seeing — solid, touchable actual objects. Our mind places the leaves on the tree and, perhaps even more clever, places the trees under and about the leaves to hold them up.

(If so, what releases the leaves, come autumn? Do we think them down? I do not believe it.)

By the same kind of description, what is out there is molecular doings, subatomic buzzings and hurryings about and under, and lots and lots and lots and lots of empty space in what our eyes and brains (&c) trick us into thinking solid.

Surely that or some such description is in some respect true. The scientific work has verified the subatomic and the perceptual apparatus alike. Hence the description is scientific and Kantian at once. Only, it's not Kantian enough, for to Kant the 'out there' is an individual intuitum for each person and also a category of the mind.[2] Say that, and the description we have tried to envisage puffs a curl of smoke and is where?

Well, *where's* in or of the mind. Can we start from there? Where's there?

The description I have given as though we could see, from, say, fifty feet to one side angled off between person and tree, a man, with visible face, eyes, hands looking out on a submicroscopic buzzing and scurrying (which we can magnify in imagination till we imagine we see it — think of cloud chambers, photographs of something actual),[3] and then we imagine the man pushing something (what?) out — projecting — until we can now see the normal tree as his mental construction. But that picture, including second observer, is itself some kind of picture, and that in turn? Is the regress we now have of imagined observers sensible? foolish? But sensible or foolish, what is being seen or imagined by whom where and how, in the description?

The second observer (as the third and so on, if relevant) has literally 'taken leave of his senses' and hence there is nothing really to imagine or describe. We can say that the scientific account and the normal account both make some sense, function somehow together, and we even say or try to say that the scientific view underlies (somehow) the normal one. But how can we trust (granting we do trust, in some way) the scientific account, which was based very firmly in a trust of the veracity of experience? Insofar as it shows experience non-veracious, is it not undercutting itself and its own presumptions?

Note well, though, that in all the vanishings, beauty vanishes no more than the rest of the experienced world, so it won't serve to use half-and-vaguened versions of such analysis to dismiss beauty as subjective. Color-blind persons don't see the colors very well. Aesthetically blind persons don't see the beauty very well.

And, then, God never promised we wouldn't find the world puzzling.

Hume, in the passage I discussed in the second chapter, was dealing with a world partially half-dissolved by such (half)-analysis, and was trying at once to boast his modernity and discoveries, *and* to rescue morality and aesthetics from the dissolution.

Trying to talk about the two accounts and to visualize both is a plain mistake, but a hard one to avoid. The magnified photographs are of actuality. But the world does not look that way; it looks, and in some real and stubborn way is, the ways it is given us to see, touch, walk about in, climb, and love. We cannot change it at our whim, but only and slightly by submitting to its rules, the way things are. It is not all of reality (mankind has needed no new science to know that levels of reality exist), and we do not need subtle instrumentations to know that our experience of the world and our perceiving are closely kin. When we close our eyes, the world as sight disappears.

The world is very open, sometimes puzzling, and very stubborn. At the base of our experiences is a deep trust in the veracity of our experience, and the recognition that our experience can be well or badly conceived, seen, known. Without the faith in the veracity of experience (and it is a faith — reason cannot get a step to stand below it or a basement to found it on), we cannot even be sceptical or ask questions. Hence scepticism presumes fidelity. As does truth.

People join, are in, are of, and transcend the physical world. The very analyses that cast doubt presume value, the possibility of reasoning, the veracity of experience.

The analysis of subject-object unties the world, at once, with no need for scientific information or Kantian subtlety. When one thinks (wrongly) as a subject over against an object, and then removes the *against*, leaving the subject really detached from the object, then perception is instantly impossible and objects instantly unknowable. So is it when we make the object of perception a percept in our minds.[4] Subject and object are awkward and poor concepts, but at least can stumble along some; pure subject and pure object are unthinkable concepts which, half unthought upon, multiply strangeness in a hall of empty mirrors where nothing can be seen, and no one can arrlve to see. Some negation is strange; but those negations are not strange, but simply the result of attempting to use concepts which, by the first gesture of establishing them, cannot work.

Let us not allow anyone to take, prematurely, the colors from the leaves, or the beauty from the trees, or the trees from the world. Let's leave things where they belong, the way things are.

8

Subjective — Objective

Subjective is biased, smudgy, bad, unscientific, untrustworthy, unfair. *Objective* is impartial, clean, good, scientific, trustworthy, fair. Such are not only connotations, suggestions of the words, but what the words mean, in much discourse. An embattled vague humanist can fuss back some, with one of the words, and call the 'objective' the 'inhuman, cold, impersonal, heartless' or such, but the other word is too infected to do much with: to call the 'subjective' the 'human, warm, personal, good-hearted' is a belligerence that sounds wrong. The scales are loaded against the shift.

The words are evaluative words, sprung from a false philosophical analysis and polemically bent to emotive suasion. Hardly a fair or sound, much less 'objective' procedure.

We hear such statements as "knowledge is cool, dispassionate, objective, testable by the very rules which have produced that knowledge. What cannot be so tested cannot lay claim to the august title of knowledge. It is simply too private because it is particular, emotive, and personal."[1] Such a view reflects a widespread attitude: the simplest, garden spade kind of empiricism, and assumes the clear distinction between fact and value, with evidence for the former and none for the latter, topics already much spoken of in this book. What here is especially pertinent is the evaluative language; rhetorically strengthened: "cool," "august" and such. The polemics of the attitude contradicts the presumed objectivity.

Such polemics is not merely added from time to time: it's locked-in to the logical structure of the terms *objective* or *subjective*, hid, self-inconsistent (evaluating evaluative judgment as inferior to value-free procedures), and hence unjust.

Objectivity is (very strangely) used to name a construct of related virtues. A person is called 'objective' who is fair, not bent towards a specific answer or party by irrelevant considerations, who is passionately determined to strive for truth, who is disciplined to submit to the evidence and reasoning by appropriate methods. Those are sound and important virtues, especially in a person who is not bent by a warped view of objectivity to ignore much real and valuable evidence. Such discipline and passion are highly valuable traits: to call them 'objective' is tangledly self-inconsistent, since the objective extrudes all value, is simon-pure-and-simple description, strongly suggesting (in many contexts, implying) that value is extra-descriptive, subjective, unknowable. By its implications, then, the notion of objectivity as a virtue undercuts and destroys itself.

One can claim some middle ground, saying something like 'Of course we don't mean the totally objective in speaking of objectivity', but the pull of the poles is powerfully felt — the magnets are heavy, and for good reason: the first move that establishes the terms is a separating, and is wrong.

One also hears such statements, for instance in praising a dean or a judge, 'he applies the rules objectively', by which is meant he applies the rules fairly, consistently, impartially. The words *objective, objectively, objectivity*, are unnecessary in such contexts, since there are good synonyms, which do not mislead, whose use might lead to clearer thought. If someone thinks he is being subjective when he considers individual features of the instance to which he is applying rules, he is very apt not to so consider; but it is a first principle of sound casuistry that one should observe what is relevantly individual in applying rules.

Feeling is always an element of judgment and sometimes is and should be an important ingredient; it need not falsify at all. A good counselor should be thoughtful, impartial, clear-headed about relevant principles, not given to emotions that confuse his judgment; *and* should be sympathetic, open, not cold-blooded, concerned. The concepts of the objective and the subjective do not fit such situations, and cannot be made to fit, both because of their potent emotional loadings (which might be eased or cured by linguistic therapy, so to speak) and because of their logical ill-formedness, which is not curable.

How could one be completely objective, make completely objective judgments, about anything? By ceasing to be a subject (person) making judgments? No judgment. By separating the objects of judgment wholly from the judgment? No judgment.

If a person making a judgment is a subject, and if that about which he makes the judgment is the object of that judgment, then every judgment is entirely subjective, since made by a subject, and every judgment is entirely objective, since entirely made about an object. One cannot save that oddity by saying that judgments are partially subjective and partially objective, since that would mean the subject made only part of the judgment he makes, and the object would be the object only in part of the judgment, all of which, by the prior definition, is about the object. Can we then be content to say that, every judgment is entirely subjective and entirely objective? What happens to the distinction? How then can one judgment be more objective than another?

A chemist doing a good job is not being objective; he's being a chemist doing a good job. He is not being more objective or less objective, either. Were the word *objective* dismissed from the language, he would not do the job one whit differently. He attends to the relevant aspects of what he is dealing with, he ignores the irrelevant aspects, he may worry some about exactly what is and is not relevant though he has stout habits and dispositions and procedures to help him there, he does the experiments and checks what he can, he compiles data, he puzzles about results, he creatively thinks and imagines new ways of looking, he gets hunches for hypotheses to test out, he suddenly sees relations he missed before, he does whatever the job requires. He refuses the temptation to push the interpretation of data towards a conclusion it almost neatly fits. In that, he's not being objective; he's resisting a temptation. He doesn't cheat, to save himself time or to swipe a little glory. In that he is not being objective, he's being good. He's doing his job.

To deal with, to think about, to judge, is normally to attend to aspects, and one can think about such processes as treating-as-objects, objectifying. But that's misleading. A surgeon does not treat the person on whom he is operating as an object, though he does not treat that person significantly as a realtor or as the second cousin of a friend. As surgeon he is not attending, significantly, to realtor-ing or degrees of consanguinity and connections thereto. But he had better treat the person as a person, secondly, as a human being who deserves careful treatment, careful paying-attention-to, to whom the surgeon is obligated by the rules of being a physician, and firstly, as a person physiologically. Courses in The Physiology of Objects are of small service to surgeons. A surgeon needs to know human anatomy and be able to connect some things back where they go.

It's natural enough when we talk of perception or judgment or such to have general terms for perceiver and perceiv-ee, for judge and that-judged-about, and the words *subject* and *object* may have some comparatively innocent uses there. The phrase "object of my affections" does not conjure up the dilemmas and misconstruings, and does not sound coldly distant and scientific. But the innocence is comparative, and care is advised, especially since the language holds some peculiar twists nearby. For instance, the subject of a book is what the book is about.

One frequent and sensible use of the word *object* expresses, mostly, our ignorance. 'What is the object in the road there?' 'I can't tell: it could be a dead animal or a piece of a truck tire'. We mean a *that*, we don't know what yet. We drive nearer, and learn. We are not referring to a class of beings each of which is sometimes a dead animal and sometimes a piece of truck tire.

Another example is an actual one from World War II. "What is that object being tracked on sonar at a constant speed and near-collision course? An American submarine? A Japanese submarine? A whale?" (We'll never know; it went its way.)

UFOs (unidentified flying objects) are often talked about as a definite class for which UFO is the correct name. Are there UFOs? Many, many thousands, since a person often cannot tell at first glance whether he is seeing a plane, a helicopter, a bird, a hang-glider ("What a strange bird!"), or something else. Are some of them very unusual objects indeed? That is a different question.

The subjective-objective dividings infiltrate and warp our language in many ways. Academic tests are called 'subjective' (essay) or 'objective' (short answer, multiple choice, or such), as though one test as much as another was not a means for a teacher to judge (evaluate) how well a student is doing in a certain course of study at a certain level. Much meta-discussion of scientific procedures and of literary criticism concern how subjective or objective science or literary criticism is or should be. Such discussion can have some value, but the questions are basically misconceived. Science is not subjective or objective in any clear sense(s); literary criticism is not subjective or objective in any clear sense(s) — simply and involvedly because the words-which-would-be-concepts *subjective* and *objective* lack clear sense. What is real in the questions can still be addressed and pondered about.

For instance, in literary criticism does fashion or personal bias sometimes worsen judgment? Yes, sometimes. Does a good literary critic need as basic equipment, fundamental tools of the trade, strong emotions, a deep power to respond imaginatively as well as thoughtfully to literary works? Yes, indeed, and unapologetically. Do the sciences teach us truth? Yes. Important truth? Yes. The only truth we can or do have? No. Are there some special problems in method and metaphysics for the sciences, and especially the social sciences? Yes. Will more data and better statistics *qua* statistics solve those problems? No. Are they simple problems? How tell, until they are solved, if they are to be solved? Are the words *subjective* and *objective* essential or even useful for discussing the real problems? No. Do *subjective* and *objective* badly distort our questioning, answering, and thinking? Yes.

Sweep them away, and let us attend to our tasks.

9

Of Some Theories: Goodness and Being

Is goodness a natural property or a non-natural property? The answer, in my judgment, to that question which has vexed and behassled much philosophizing, is 'Both', 'Neither', and (mostly) 'No, thank you'. The question is mis-asked, the concepts mis-conceived, hence there cannot be an answer, strictly, to it. Insofar as the concepts get anywhere, 'both' and 'neither' are both correct answers to some things the questions struggles at. Primarily, the question is to be rejected.

Why? Because nature, as presumed in the question, is a realm of mere Fact, pure object, a realm utterly extruded of value, utterly describably and verifiable (that is, evaluated) without any evaluation. The realm does not exist. Since there is no such nature, and cannot be such a nature — and if there could be such a nature, our language would be entirely incompetent to say any word about it — there cannot be any natural properties. One could say, in a spirit of some niggling, that since the nature intended is non-existent, then all properties whatever are non-natural properties, properties quite detached from that empiric, mis-imagined, unimaginable, inconceivable 'nature'.

The moves go on and on, over and over: take value wholly out (try to) by an evaluation of the world which excludes value and evaluation, and then either boast that value cannot be found or try varying ways to bridge back from the world-so-conceived to value, which cannot be done from the first move conceiving the world as mere fact.

We do not attend to every aspect of reality, even every aspect of reality we know about, in making a given judgment. What is not attended to does not thereby vanish from the world. Out of sight, out of mind, out of where? The physicist does not attend to certain moral evaluations in doing his experiments, making his imaginative leaps, constructing physics, but he had better attend with exquisite courtings to a difficult and elaborate *moral* and *intellectual* discipline, namely, doing physics *well*. If one meant by empiricism, not attending to some aspects of reality part of the time, it would be fine, but empiricism comes to mean playing-like the aspects not-attended-to part of the time are not there any of the time, even though the empiricist assumes that they are in his very philosophical claiming of empiricism.

Goodness cannot be a natural property if (1) natural properties are all matter-of-fact, (2) value is excluded by definition or strong suggestion from matter-of-fact. But, on that reckoning, natural properties are value-less by definition, hence worth-less, and cannot be known since knowledge is (1) valuable (2) always involves evaluation.

Nor is the word-and-concept(s) *property* very helpful.

Is a property any trait? an essential or distinguishing trait? Are adjectives in the business of naming or being properties? A property is, by its history, something that belongs to or is owned by some person or thing, but there are many ways of owning or belonging or being-related-to.

The clarity (philosophical-respectability) of *property* is, I suspect, an illusion. In any event, until we are lucidly certain, or reasonably so, what a property is or means, why make much of questions which require a grasp of the concept?

Peter Geach sums up three theories vis-a-vis the relation of goodness to good-making attributes.

"Now the relation between goodness and the attribute that makes a thing good has been an intractable puzzle to modern philosophers. Broadly speaking, they have three types of theory: (i) an identification of goodness, by definition, with some particular good-making attribute (theories of this sort are said by their opponents to exemplify the 'naturalistic fallacy'); (ii) a view that the adjective 'good' in its primary acceptation has commendatory or prescriptive, not descriptive, force; (iii) a view that goodness is an odd 'non-natural' attribute, united by a queer (non-logical and non-casual) 'must' to the good-making characteristics.

In my opinion all three turn out to be blind alleys."[1]

The foregoing discussion should show why (ii) and (iii) are blind alleys. It is not goodness that is odd, as in (iii); what is odd is the mis-structure of 'nature' underlying 'natural property'; the adjective *good* and related words of evaluation certainly have descriptive — that is, real — force and everyone, off philosophical duty, knows that.[2] We commend an action because we believe it to be a good action; we prescribe a course of action because we believe it really should be done. To reverse that logical order is indeed odd, not to say perverse, a twisting-back necessitated by the logical hump of matter-of-factness as conceived in the empiricist tradition, where the term 'descriptive' can only refer to value-neutral and value-neutered 'matter-of-fact', leaving value out, by primary move, from that 'world'.

Can one identify goodness with any good-making attribute? That question admits perils, answered Aye or Nay.

Aquinas identifies goodness and (fullness of) being,[3] an inherently plausible identification or relation. Something realizes its being when it fulfills the function of the sort of being that it can truly come to be. A sharp knife is a good knife because it cuts better. Exceptions may qualify the point: an electrician's knife must not be too sharp or it will cut wire as well as insulation. That keeps us from treating sharpness as the only or even the essential quality of a knife's being, as does the recognition that a knife must have some organized parts and structures with a range of logistical demands. Butter knives made of butter would not work very well. A knife's moderately complex being constitutes its goodness, its power to do its job. Sharpness does not define a knife, but is an important constituent of the definition and the function.

That identification also works negatively, at least to some degree. A three-legged raccoon is not a separate zoological species but a defective raccoon. The defect is precisely a failure of being, of not being what a full-formed raccoon is. Certainly the concepts of being, function, the realization and fulfillment of chosen or natural ends, are very important concepts in moral and aesthetic thinking and in human action.

So far, so well, one hopes. But rough winds can rise. For instance, mean folks not fond of raccoons could say some things.

'Three-legged raccoons are *better* than four-legged raccoons; they do less mischief; a three-legged raccoon is less apt than a four-legged raccoon to steal campers' fare'.

'The only good raccoon is a dead raccoon'.

Or, by someone who preferred the looks of the raccoon to its actions: 'The only good raccoon is a stuffed raccoon'.

Goodness of function has to do with fulfilling function, achieving relevant ends, but choices exist between ends and people disagree about the intrinsic worth of ends, including whether ends *have* intrinsic worth, and the problems are not simply solvable by an appealing to the identification of goodness and being. To attempt to reconcile the differences by appealing to the quantity of being leads rapidly to the problems of utilitarianism. To attempt to reconcile by appealing to quality of being surrenders instantly the identification of being and goodness, since it presumes standards apart from degrees of being. If goodness just is being, how can some kinds of being have higher degrees of goodness than others?

The problems, though complex, may be manageable, and Aquinas can handsomely take care of himself, but a severer problem, frequently pointed out, remains: One *understands* the denial of the identification, and, in a peculiar way, to understand that denial is to admit the denial.

William Butler Yeats translates a stanza from Sophocles as follows:

"Never to have lived is best, ancient writers say;
    Never to have drawn the breath of life, never to have looked
        into the eye of day;
    The second best's a gay goodnight and quickly turn away."[4]

One may and should deny that denial, however attractive the poetry makes it sound, but still the meaning of the denial is clear: "Never to have lived is best." Were the identification of goodness and being the meaning of the concept goodness, the sentence would mean, 'Never to have had any being is to have more being than to have some being', which is self-inconsistent and senseless. But the assertion in the poem is not senseless; it asserts a conflict between Thomistic views and the hedonistic calculus (the terms are anachronistic vis-a-vis Sophocles, but not the thought). If hedonism is true, and pleasure is the good and pain (in all senses, not just the strong senses) the bad, then a life in which pain (disgratification) predominates over pleasure (gratification) gets a minus score, and is thus, by the premise, clearly worse than a never-having-been-born-life, which gets a score of zero. Or one could give other than hedonistic reasons (or give no reasons) and still assert, "Never to have been born is best," and be, in some real way, understood.

Thus the meaning of the term goodness and the term being cannot be identical. We clearly grasp the concept good even when we struggle, unavailingly, to define it exactly. The reason for the unsuccess to define may well be that the concept good, like the concept truth, is a fundamental concept, and we cannot get under it to define it, much less, despite some recent attempts, to get rid of it. The concept is one of the most fundamental means by which we grasp the world.

If goodness were identified, by definition, with one attribute, then the term and concept of goodness would be totally expendable, as redundant, and when some one said 'Goodness is pleasure', 'Goodness is being', 'Goodness is obedience to God' or whatever, what would be offered would be pure tautology: 'being is 'being', 'pleasure is pleasure', 'obedience to God is obedience to God',[5] which is not what the identifier is contending.

But an identifier can still contend, and it is really what is frequently intended, that while the term 'good' has a graspable meaning other than 'pleasure', goodness really does consist of pleasure and nothing else, or goodness consists wholly of being or obedience-to-God or whatever. That's contrary to common sense, which certainly thinks that many things are good, and that a good person is good because he has many namable good (and good-making) attributes. But common sense may be wrong, or ill-instructed; and even where common sense is right in detail, it is possible that the many it holds as good may reduce to one. Of such questions I shall have something more to say.

Meanwhile, let us take an excursus to a mountain scene.

10

Excursus:
In the Mountains

Witness.   I was an eyewitness. I saw Foxy Mentone murder Tom
   Boxfitt.

Philosopher.   No, you couldn't see that. You saw Foxy Mentone kill
   Tom Boxfitt, but the murder wasn't out there where he killed
   him; the murder was just a sentiment of blame you felt inside.

W.   Hmmnh. I would have sworn I saw that. You mean, when I saw
   Foxy kill Tom he wasn't murdering him?

P.   No, that's not what I mean. I mean that you inferred the murder,
   you figured it out, since you couldn't see it. Murder is not there
   to see.

W.   Wasn't much to figure out. I saw it, right there on the rock ledge.
   You mean he murdered Tom somewhere else, not on the ledge
   of rock? And what is this 'not there to see'?

P.   No, not somewhere else. Not anywhere. You can't be a *witness* to
   a murder, since murder involves intent, and intent is invisible.

W.   He didn't murder him *anywhere*? That's mighty peculiar. I think.
   Anyway, I must be able to witness intent, because I did, in court.
   Several of us saw Foxy in the beer hall and heard him say that
   he was going to kill Tom because Tom had been messing around
   with Susie Blaine and had smart-talked Foxy too.

P.   Er, excuse me. Tom Boxfitt wasn't a philosopher, was he?

W.   Oh, no, sir. Not that kind of smart-talk. Don't you worry a bit.

P.   Umm, yes. But, you see, you didn't witness the intent either. You
   inferred it from his conversation.

W.   I suppose.

P.   Now we're getting some place. Let's grant that he had a motive. Still the motive can't be seen. It's inside the man.

W.   I didn't think it was up a pine tree or something.

P.   That admits the point. It's not murder unless there is motive and intent, and neither motive nor intent can be seen, so murder can't be seen, can't be witnessed.

W.   Well, I did witness in court, sworn in and everything. But, if what you say is right, I didn't witness no killing neither. You can't see a man die. Death is inside a man, mighty still. You can't hear a man talk, because talk has meaning in it and you can't hear meanings. I reckon you can't witness anything, at least the way you're talking about seeing and hearing and such.

P.   Well, that's going a bit far. The real point is verifiability, evidence, telling whether something is so or not, on the basis of facts. So you can verify that one man kills another, but there's no way to verify murder, because the notion of murder involves both fact and moral or legal principle, and only what is entirely factual can be verified. There cannot be any evidence for what's not factual; and I know that's so because I don't count as evidence anything except what pertains to what I call fact [why did I let that slip out?]. So there can't be evidence for murder.

W.   Why, what was the trial all about? No evidence! Me and my two hunting buddies plain saw it happen, and there was a lot of witnesses to intent, and motive, and trouble between the two men before, and the lawyers argued and the jury decided, and the judge ruled, and Foxy got twenty years in the slammer. Some folks thought that was too light and some folks thought it was too heavy. Folks do disagree about things. But nobody disagreed about it being first-degree murder; everybody knew he had done it, and planned it ahead of time.

P.   Well, yes, in a sense. There's fact and there's law, and the law is applied to the facts and a decision is reached. But there's no evidence for law; it's just passed. There is evidence that a man is legally guilty. And besides, proving a man is legally guilty doesn't prove him morally wrong. Positive law and morality are separate, autonomous realms.

W.   You've said a bunch of things, but you sure have changed your mind about what evidence is in a hurry. A minute ago you said it was just about fact, and now it's available for applying law to fact. That's some shift. And besides, if I didn't think murder was wrong I wouldn't have come forward to testify. I didn't have to. And legislators sure think there's evidence for and against a law they're considering passing. They argue about what is better and worse. And, besides, if I saw a man at all, or blood flow — colored the color of blood — I saw Foxy Mentone murder Tom Boxfitt. I tell you, stranger. You sure do talk funny about things; you must have worked at it. A long time.

11

Language as Evaluation

Language is, I have been urging, evaluative through and through. Language realizes values, as ends, to fulfill actualities, to recognize truth, to express feelings, to amuse, to perform other functions. Functions are fulfilled *well* or *badly*. Human beings seek ends as good, and judge how well or how imperfectly ends are fulfilled. Whatever else man may be — emotional, rationalizing, mortal, brutish, reasonable, whatever — he is very much a teleological animal. He makes; he tries to get things done; he seeks to do and to understand, understanding being an activity with its own end (understanding sought intrinsically) and with related, instrumental, or other goods. Fulfilling ends depends on the nature of the fulfiller and the fulfill-ee. The acorn strives to oakhood, fails early or succeeds in becoming an oak, an oak spindly, diseased, wind-bent, undergrown, mature, or magnificent. The possibilities are very many, and frequently mysterious. Do acorns really strive? That sounds odd; yet they surely are not purely passive, billiard balls a-bouncing off extrinsic causes. The teleological is interior, to unfold, to increase, to strive. Seeds cannot be blind, or see. The intellectual as the botanical harvest is inexact. Genetics explains, and that curiously as well as intricately: of genetic codes, of information. That is (so to speak?), acorns talk their way to oaks. Or, a little more poetically perhaps (but not thereby false), acorns sing a tune to themselves which becomes their growth. The rhythms, and sequencings, and mystery are real.

Linguistic use is motivated (whether a given motive is personal, universal, self-expressive, noble, trivial, whatever). People do not happen at random to say at random sounds that happen to be words that happen to constitute sentences and paragraphs. To be motivated

91

is to seek to fulfill ends and to seek to fulfill the end(s) well, fulfillingly, which is to treat the end as a good.

Language is through and through evaluative, value-laden, value-founded, value-presuming, value-seeking, value-structured. Hence the notion of mere fact, pure description, is a delusion, a persistent and deep delusion much hammered at and exemplified away in these pages. Philosophers have got into the habit of talking of 'brute facts'. Yes, facts are subhuman, under-the-reach-of-value and evaluation, which is why people can't say any facts. Brutes are dumb. To the degree that other animals get themselves something like-or-near language, to that degree they have ceased to be brutes.

G. E. M. Anscombe writes of degrees of brutishness of facts and gives some examples.[1] But, if there are degrees of brutishness of facts, then there are no brute facts (just plain brute facts, facts *simpliciter*), only facts in which the human perpetrators are striving to subhumanize, disenvalue their facts and variously failing. If they were to succeed, they would (1) cease being human, (2) stop speaking. The drive toward monistic empiric description is powerful, but inherently impossible of realization.[2] To the degree to which it is in some vague sense possible (in a stricter sense it is not possible at all) and achieved, to that degree the achieving of facticity would be an achievement, a fulfillment, and as such non-factual.

Discussion or thinking or judging about any topic requires attending-to, an appropriate attending-to (which truth is itself an important moral truth), and what constitutes the appropriateness is an act of judgment. Since we are not God, we need to restrict our attention. The astronomer viewing the rings of Saturn in order to do certain specific things (say, a kind of measuring or spectral analysis) will, *qua* astronomer-at-that-moment, ignore the beauty of what he sees through the telescope, though he may well not be an astronomer at all and well may not be the best sort of astronomer if he never has responses (true emotional judgments) of delight and awe at the majesty of the starry skies. Many other thoughts or judgments he could or may have are richly irrelevant to what he's doing — for instance, about the quality of his laboratory assistant's manners at table. If such judgments distract, to that degree the astronomer is less able as astronomer. Yet his laboratory assistant's manners in the laboratory procedures (e.g. the bad habit of trying to clean delicate parts with a greasy and gritty rag) may be vitally relevant, even for some equipment fatally relevant. Contrarily, someone can make a moral judgment about adultery without having a cardiogram of each of the parties on each occasion.

It is hard to say what is wholly irrelevant. Table manners, insofar as they show carelessness, could be relevant to a judgment of an assistant as assistant. 'If he's that careless and inconsiderate outside of the observatory, can he always be trusted to be meticulous at his tasks within the observatory? Perhaps, but at least a shade of doubt may reasonably enter my mind.' One should be considerate of other human beings — a highly general moral truth (natural law).

What is true in what the empiricist sees about science is a good bit: methods, results, discipline, the exclusion from consideration a number of possible judgments and issues. But to assume thereby that those procedures of science are value-neutral is false, and untrue (unfaithful) to science itself. Science is valuable because of virtuous achievement of a difficult kind. A scientific observer is never mere observer, select though he must, since it is the requirements and disciplines and fulfillment of science that sets the parameters and habits of observing. That's true of pure science — the very adjective 'pure' suggests the valid ideal of knowledge conceived as a good; and true as much for the investigators at work on something where human choice, morality, valuing, set the end and some of the terms: e.g., cancer research.

The notion of value-neutrality (facticity) is simply the notion, valid in itself, of selection and exclusion of what is attended to. The push for it to mean something quite (and indefensibly and self-defeatingly) other is the mistake.

Ray Lepley, in *The Verifiability of Value*, begins with the distinction between fact and value, between the objective and subjective, and furthermore is intent on applying "the experimental outlook"[3] of "scientific knowing"[4] to ethics. I do not believe that 'the experimental outlook' is a sufficiently coherent concept, since there are many methods, including experiments (or analogies to experiments) in many disciplines, and since science and other knowledge is prior to epistemology.

Yet Lepley uses his 'experimental' methods quite flexibly and intelligently, and in the process undoes the fact-value knottedness. Instead of assuming that values cannot be verified and badgering and distorting all sorts of evidence to fit that assumption, he actually looks

at real examples and finds that value often can be verified and that
doing so is one of the most common and successful of human activities.
He ends by denying, in a strong sense, the whole fact-value, descriptive-
evaluative distinction; in the following statements.

> "Each kind of statement — whether scientific, aesthetic, or moral
> — can then be made in more factual or in more valuative terms
> and in any case transposed without alteration of essential reference
> and meaning into either of the other forms."[5]

> "[L]ike fact and value statements, the scientific, aesthetic, and moral
> may be but different modes of expression whose somewhat unique
> qualities result from the *predominant direction of attention* in each
> case. . . . However improbable this suggestion may seem to us
> because of our common habits of thinking, nonetheless it is
> apparently confirmed by examination of the transposability of these
> various kinds of statement."[6]

> "[T]he various kinds of fact and value are, each en masse, equally
> verifiable, as are all facts and values similarly compared."[7]

These conclusions, "improbable . . . to us because of our common
habits of thinking"[8] were reached by the following procedure: "Fact
and value statements and problems were . . . selected at random and
studied in relation to a scale of verifiability suggested by the empirical
[i.e., intelligent] examination of cases."[9]

> "[F]acts' and 'values,' even as commonly distinguished, vary in
> degree of verifiability from the rather definitely verifiable to the
> probably unverifiable[,] and . . . the verification . . . is at least much
> and basically the same."[10]

He also gives telling examples.

FACTS
In science: This burner will burn. This water is chemically pure.
In art: This is a tube of red paint. This space at the left of the picture
is two inches long.

In morals: This desk is fifty inches long. This is a location in which the light to this desk comes from the left.

VALUES

In science: This burner does not burn well. This water is a good solvent for this salt.

In art: This is not a good paint for this purpose. This line is too long to balance the other in this picture.

In morals: This wall-space is too short for this desk. This is the best location for this desk."[11]

Note how close the facts and values are. Fact becomes value or value fact, by a shift of attention. The facts are there for the values, for getting the jobs done. Lepley's contribution is, therefore, substantial and important.

Logic itself is value-rooted, value-realizing. One does logic *well* or *badly*. One says that thinkers have fallen into logical *confusion* or are in a conceptual *muddle*. Syllogisms themselves are called *valid* or *invalid*. Even the use of *value* in 'truth-value' is not quite accidental, not an entire pun. We wish and will and hope to do logic and argument *well*, to think clearly. We justly admire clarity and subtlety. Why? Because they are admirable. (To say that they become really admirable because we admire them, or to suggest that admiration is an emotion we project on a value-free world, is perverse.)

Gottlob Frege writes of the theory of arithmetic, "The end must be knowledge, and it must determine everything that happens."[12] To fulfill an end is good, the good which accords with the fulfilling of the end.

Frege, like many idealistic persons, can be sarcastic. He writes of that he considers a fundamental confusion in formalist theory of arithmetic, "I suppose one must infer from this that the mathematicians have a well established right to their procedure. For logicians it is otherwise."[13] It is *right* to get things right, and Frege was strongly motivated to do so.

One does not have a right to reason wrongly. It is wrong to do so. If one says that someone gets an answer right, the 'right' constitutes instant praise. It is not merely even largely a play on language, to conflate the sense of *right* (accuracy) and *right* (deserving of praise);

the senses are conflated in the words. Accuracy is praiseworthy. To reason rightly is to reason well; it is to avoid error. Frege says that logic tells us how we "ought to think."[14]

Logic is a value-laden, value-founded, value-permeated activity. So is language. In the is-ought question, the catch is in the is-statements, where the lookers almost never look, as they struggle with the ought-statements or possible or impossible bridgings in between. An assumption is "the view . . . popular in our . . . time . . . that "ought"-statements make no truth claims at all."[15] That assumption is quickly dropped in practice, since if one has a 'pro-attitude' (the very ugliness and awkwardness of the jargon is significant) towards an action, one has it because one believes that that action is *virtuous*. If one commends something, it is because one believes that that something is worth commending. To say 'I commend archery though I do not believe that that archery is worth commending' is to contradict oneself, to confess to lying, or to confess to philosophy. The real catch lies in the is-statement, in the deep, hard-to-examine belief that there plainly are is-statements, facts, mere-descriptions, which we can (valuably) know, verify, handle with comfort, statements which are utterly non-evaluative in their presumptions, content, and meaning. There are no such statements, nor can there be in our language.

The strugglers come close to seeing or saying this truth, in good glimpses; and certainly the struggle away from reductive positivism, empiricism, Hume-ism, in the last few decades offers good signs of linguistic and intellectual and moral health, not even to mention the many interesting or valuable explorations of what logic and language are and do. Yet the gap persists.

R. M. Hare writes of "certain ways of behaving, describable in perfectly neutral terms, which makes us commend people as, for example, courageous. Citations for medals. . . . give descriptive details."[16] One should commend Hare's own courage for trying to pluck out pure-description from the heart of the enemy (evaluative) camp: the language in a commendation for courageous behavior. It is a brave and nimble-footed sortie, but the quarry escapes.

There are no "perfectly neutral terms" and, if there were, our language could never speak them, because there would be no motivation to speak them; if terms are spoken or written, someone has a motive for so doing and the terms are thereby and to that degree 'tainted' with value.

Hare finds the distinction between description and evaluation an "essential tool . . . . of the philosopher."[17] I find it quite otherwise, a crude and inexact but sometimes moderately useful distinction (if we don't look too close), but an impossible distinction once-purified, which occasions all manner of havoc, including the is-ought imbroglio. Its meaning is just (or at least mostly) that we sometimes do not attend to certain aspects of meaning, implication, truth, context, or structure, and that that not-attending can have its uses. If using perfectly-neutral-description is sometimes an essential tool of the philosopher, in all such sometimes the description is not perfectly neutral, but essential-as-tool, hence infected (incurably) with value. To reply that in such an argument I am shifting from content to context (value-neutral in content, useful in context) will not serve: content depends basically, intricately, and inescapably on context. There are no perfectly neutral terms in a military commendation, because all the detail is being used to commend; there are no perfectly neutral terms anywhere else, either. Perfectly neutral terms could not get said.

What are some uses of the distinction? Rough ones. I may (do sometimes) tell a class to paraphrase and scan a poem and then, afterwards, apply what they have done in judging how good the poem is. We can say, in such a situation, that we are first *describing* the poem's meaning and meter and then *evaluating* the poem. But the whole context is of understanding (a good) and evaluation (a good) and, as activities, paraphrasing and scanning can be done well or badly. The distinction has a rough, pedagogic function, but no place in the process is actually value-neutral; and that pedagogic procedure is a little arbitrary, though defensible (again a judgment of value); much discussion combines description and evaluation more interwovenly.

Let me essay a definition, then some comments. *Description is evaluation with certain aspects of the evaluation not-attended-to.* Description is always done for reasons of value and very often for directly evaluative purposes. Description is always constituted by evaluation. It is, on analysis, description that vanishes, not evaluation.

If one means by an 'is'-statement a statement that can be true or false, then ought statements, since they can be true or false, are 'is'-statements, and the is-ought problem vanishes. If one means by an is-statement a pure description, a mere fact, then, since there are and can be no such statements in our language, the is-ought problem vanishes.

If one means by an 'is'-statement, a description (in the rough sense described above), and by an 'ought'-statement an evaluation with the word *ought* or a close synonym (*should* in some contexts, *owe, obligation* in others) or, anyway, a sentence that somehow directly and overtly conveys the notion of specific ought-ness, then many a description leads to many an evaluation (ought-statement), and many do not. J. R. Searle's showing that a statement about owing an obligation ('ought'-statement) can be derived from a statement about making a promise ('is'-statement)[18] is, in my judgment, correct, and, from the many responses to it and defenses of it, has been influential in weakening the is-ought barrier. So, historically, what he does is valuable and to be highly commended.

What it does actually, in one way, approaches the tautologous. The notion 'promise' contains the notion 'owing an obligation'; when we do not, for the moment, attend to owing-obligation, we get an 'is'-statement; when we do attend to the owing-obligation part, we get an 'ought'-statement. 'Now you see it, now you don't!' 'Why?' 'You looked away'.

Searle's derivation is in five statements, ending with these two:
"(4) Jones is under an obligation to pay Smith five dollars.
(5) Jones ought to pay Smith five dollars."[19]

One could perfectly well say that (4) is an 'is'-statement, and (5) is an 'ought'-statement derivable from (4), simply by not attending to the 'ought' notion in "obligation" in (4), and by attending to the "ought" in (5).

One can go a step further, thus:
(1) Jones ought to pay Smith five dollars ('is'-statement)
(2) Jones ought to pay Smith five dollars ('ought'-statement)

In (1) we attend to the truth, what Searle calls the "institutional fact,"[20] and not the oughtness as obligation. In (2) we attend to the ought-ness, and thus we have an 'ought'-statement.

The prescriptive statement "Jones ought to pay Smith five dollars" does not follow from the descriptive statement "Jones ought to pay Smith five dollars," if — as is typically meant — the prescriptive statement *adds* prescribing to Jones, or even *adds* commending to someone else. But what that shows is that commendation, approval, prescribing, advising, are posterior to believing a moral truth. If one advises Jones that he should fulfill an obligation to Smith, while not believing that Jones is under an obligation to do so, one is — let charity prevail — a typical victim of the confusions of empiricism. The confusions are curable; even empiricism may be. Hope is pleasurable.

Searle himself finds the empirical position, including the notion that value statements "are not capable of objective or factual truth or falsity at all,"[21] to be "very attractive,"[22] but finds that "one of the things that is wrong with it is that it fails to give us any coherent account of such notions as commitment, responsibility, or obligation."[23]

Anthony Flew, in arguing against Searle, nicely gives the whole case away. Flew quotes Popper with approval:

"Nature consists of facts and regularities, and is in itself neither moral nor immoral. It is we who impose our standards upon nature, and who introduce in this way morals into the natural world, in spite of the fact that we are part of this world. . . . *It is impossible to derive a sentence stating a norm or a decision from a sentence stating a fact*; this is only a way of saying that it is impossible to derive norms or decisions *or proposals* from facts."[24]

The gap between fact and value is absolutely absolute, value is utterly underivable from fact, yet from the realm of the absolutely and merely factual (i.e., nature) men, who are wholly part of nature and in no way transcendent, have imposed value on nature. Morals are within humanity, humanity within nature, nature contains no morals; it only contains human beings who have morals to impose. Nature consists [entirely is plainly intended] of facts and regularities, and human beings have introduced morals "into" the natural world.

Even if value were wholly illusory, the nature Popper would impose on us could never produce even the illusion of value. Hence, if people have even illusions about values, much less value, Popper's nature is non-existent.

Flew's comments are even more revealing:

"Popper's account . . . . presents the idea of the Naturalistic Fallacy as involved in the clash of world-outlooks and personal commitments

.... [T]he most relevant and important difference [between Searle's and Popper's accounts] is that Popper at least suggests, what is true, that the fundamental discrimination in terms of which the Naturalistic Fallacy is being characterised is not, and does not have to be thought to be, a clearcut feature of all actual discourse. It is not something which you cannot fail to observe everywhere as already there and given, if once you have learnt what to look for. There is, rather, a differentiation which has to be made and insisted upon; and the distinction is one the development of which may go against the grain of set habits and powerful inclinations."[25]

Even so. Language is not like that, and you won't find it so even after you have learned to try. Language is quite otherwise, but to support a world-outlook and personal commitment, the empiricist must continually redo language and distort experience in order to impose his conviction. Yes. Which is, and more so since unintended, quite a confession.

Searle writes, "The urge to read the metaphysical distinction between Fact and Value back into language as a thesis about valid entailment relations must inevitably run up against counter-examples, because speaking a language is everywhere permeated with the facts of commitments undertaken, obligations assumed, cogent arguments presented, and so on."[26]

Yes, and not just in argument. Language is evaluation.

12

Value: Realization and Ends

In this book I have pointed out, reiterated, analyzed, and urged the imprecision and elusiveness of certain concepts, notably fact, subject-object, subjective-objective, description, is-statement. In the process I have exemplified and urged the nature of language as evaluation, the ineradicable presence of value in and through language, have used a number of expressions, in some part metaphorical, such as 'value-laden', 'value-permeated', 'value-founded' and others, including a range of concepts with evident value-implications: good, ought, obligation, commendable (worthy-of-being-commended), beautiful, right. The words *beautiful* and *ought* have different grammar, functions, and meanings. To say that the statement 'the waterfall is beautiful' means the same thing as 'the waterfall is doing what it ought to do' is clearly to make a mistake, though an interesting mistake. In some sense waterfalls are beautiful in doing what they ought to do (and 'ought' to be beautiful), though they 'ought' to transfer water downward also. Fulfilling of function is crucial, perhaps basic, in understanding what ought to be; hence the words *ought* and *beautiful* are important evaluative words, with inter-connectings.

Variants of meaning within the same word have also been noted: 'Truth-value' as a logical term is not identical with the broader meaning of the term 'value', though the connections matter; so for 'logically right' and 'morally right'.

Do such concepts have a class essence common to all or to something-in-all, perhaps a part of feature of all? Do they have family resemblances (in the Wittgensteinian, now-much-used metaphor)?[1] If so, do they, on one side of the family, have a direct descent from a forefather, perhaps entitling them to membership in the Sons of the American Revolution?

101

Families are kin of blood; the metaphor of family resemblance is not of merely casual overlapped likenesses.

We use words better than we define them, and sometimes it is a debater's trick (or sincere philosophic confusion) to demand definition.[2] 'What do you mean by the word *value*? Until you give me a clear univocal, universally agreed-on definition, the discussion cannot proceed'.

To such a query one might reply, 'Fair enough. I shall as soon as you define the word *the* as used in your question, in clear, abstract, univocal terms without examples or synonyms. And don't say it is a definite article, because that begs the question by presuming we have grammatical knowledge and experience of sentences. We'll proceed when you comply'.

To which could be responded, 'Fair enough. I shall as soon as you define three words in your most recent sentence'.

Beginning that discussion would take a while.

We use language, well or badly. We cannot get behind language in order to define 'well' and 'badly' before we say the first word; in language we grasp concepts and do much else. To grasp a concept is to grasp it, directly. A child recognizes a cat and says "cat," a feat impossible to paraphrase or to reduce to some abstract or abstracted definition the child has been taught. We do think. Once we have learned how, we grasp many a concept without mediation; and if a concept is basic to our thought, then we cannot get under it or behind it to found it on other terms, analyses, or definitions. The concepts of value and truth are basic, hence — in what should be a necessarily lucid sense — indefinable.[3] How the basic sense is incorporated (in-concept-ed) in the other uses is more complex.

Imagine a conversation:

> 'Define *should*'.
>   'I won't. Why should I?'
>   'Why should you? Of course you should!
>   You can't lay claim to being reasonable
>   if you don't'.

Is the conversation playfully intended? A little. Still, the point is there. No one can ever claim that there is an obligation to define the word *obligation* without admitting — directly or covertly — that he already knows what the word means.

We speak morally, ethically, aesthetically, evaluatively because we already grasp what such terms mean and imply, what a basic notion of value is, and a fit sense at least of how the basic, grasped sense is and moves in various terms: 'ought', 'good', 'evaluative' and such.[4] We begin there. We have begun there. Our language and our language acts are steeped in evaluation, recognizing what is of value, realizing good, seeking truth as a good, discriminating justly, deciding between meanings, analyzing to clarify, all the rest. Language is an activity; activities are fulfillment of potentialities according to an end or ends conceived of, grasped as good. It is no accident of language that we speak of ends sought as good, even when we speak of economic goods. Such a move is very close to the substance of language, and the reality and experience that language manifest. Since empiricism must adopt, use, and deal with language so to construct its case, and since empiricism in content flatly denies that there is value or truth of value, yet must assume and use the reality it denies at every point of its operations, empiricism is incoherent and incompatible with the real world. What is compatible with language and experience? The reality of value. 'But to admit that much is to open the door towards theism, toward Christianity'. Yes. It opens it wide, an opening which explains some of the fierce resistance to the move.

To discuss all the moves of the envaluing in language exceed my patience and wit, but some are worth noting. 'If you want to catch the four o'clock bus, you ought to leave in the next ten minutes'. The 'ought' does not have the directly moral sense, but the connection is real. We should (ought to) realize our lawful ends (the cardinal virtue of prudence), other things being equal, hence, if the "want" is a legitimate desire not outweighed by other desires or considerations, and if the judgment involving time is right, then one indeed ought to leave within the time. Other things and desires are often not equal. Restricting our desires for good reason (sometimes, practice in restraint is a good reason) is very important in our moral and spiritual lives, and a number of things are more important than desiring (e.g., needing, caring). Still, a moral sense *is* present in the 'ought' in such a sentence.

What about doing things just for fun? Doing (innocent) things just for fun (other things being equal) is a very *good* reason for doing things, realizing a pure, non-instrumental delight in some activity, a pure and delightful form of realization, of fulfillment of function. Hence doing things just for fun is not really doing them just for fun, since we are not merely serving ourselves and our delight, but concentrating on the activity. The delight comes from the activity. Further, except possibly for some very extraordinary people, it is a very important duty to do some things, relatively trivial things, 'just for fun', since otherwise we become tense, uncooperative, grouchy, and fail in the virtue of Complaisance (in Thomas Hobbes's sense),[5] in agreeable cooperation with others. To take the 'just' in 'just for fun' too seriously leads, therefore, to inconsistency. But it's better ethics and better psychology (as often the two overlap) not to take the 'just' too seriously or the duty too solemnly. That way, delight is more fun.

The concept good does some ranging, mostly connected (it would take some ingenuity to bring "Good grief!" into the fold), and very largely connected by teleology, the realization of ends, the fulfillment of function: a good knife, a good baseball player, a good sonata, a good worker, a good time, even the indirect and mildly complex functions implicit in a wished "good night." It is good to get things done; it is good to relax, to enjoy living (is that not getting good things done?).

'Ah, but knives are used for armed robbery! and metaphorical knives for mean academic back-stabbing'. Yes. A gun is even *better* for armed robbery than a knife because it's immediately safer (harder to wrest away from you, more apt to keep the victim from running away) but *worse* than a knife for armed robbery because it is apt to get you a worse punishment and much more apt to get you immediately killed if a policeman catches you in the act. Hence one decides, on balance (rationally or impulsively) of those and other considerations whether to use a gun or a knife in an armed robbery. And if you want to be truly *good* at mean academic back-stabbing you *ought* to develop a ready tongue and a deceitful heart.

That is, human activities have structures and logistics and what one ought to do depends on those structures and logistics to fulfill the ends involved. The end in both armed robbery and academic back-stabbing includes self-punishment, achieving the thrill of self-hatred, and, as in many other human activities, many a tangle of motive. The human heart!

What makes certain ends evil is the failure to fulfill more valid ends, and the frustration of other legitimate ends of other people. The Golden Rule is not optional, not a principle one may, with equal rightness, choose or deny. People are people, with capacities for good and evil, and one may not treat them otherwise. Armed robbery, at least for small sums on the street, is largely stupid, a failure of intelligence to provide for oneself, a violation of prudence. So is academic back-stabbing, at heart.

'A good third-baseman can be a very immoral man'.

Yes, but there are limits, affected by his third-basemenship. He can be conceited, contentious, licentious, uncooperative, self-indulgent, but he cannot play competently without staying in some kind of physical shape (which sets a limit to self-indulgence), and, however uncooperative or self-willed he is off the field, he cannot be either extrinsically in the act of starting a double play. His heart does not have to be in the right place, but his hands better be. Should he, because he is angry at the second baseman, field a ball and not throw it when there is a good opportunity for a double play, he is being a bad third baseman, a bad man and a bad creature (because his fellow players, the management, and the spectators are real people with whom he has entered actual and moral contracts, and since the Summary of the Law is not optional). In truth he would not be a third baseman at all, and, assuming he survived the crowd's ire, his contract would be revoked. By choosing to be a non-third-baseman he would justly become an ex-third-baseman.

Since baseball is not the highest good, one can imagine exceptions in which the act would be good. Perhaps he is playing in East Berlin (or Stalag 17) and the ensuing riot would allow a number of people to escape. Bad thirdbasemanship would then become heroic virtue (a judgment which presumes the rightness of his cause).

Ends are grasped and sought as good. Since there is choice of various ends, some ends are more important than others, and choices can, should, and must be made between ends. What is good as fulfilling an end may be bad in larger context. Yet that surely does not mean that the term 'good' is being used equivocally. It is being used functionally and decisively.

What do works of art do? Various good and bad things. They please and gratify audiences; they instruct; they turn our souls toward the

beautiful; they achieve formal excellence; they express feeling; they
clarify, they gratify (not infrequently unduly) artists making them. The
fairly common modern aesthetics which substitutes 'process' for
'product' has a point, but essentially a perverse point. One is not doing
the process unless one is trying to achieve a good product. That is
what the process is. A parallel is that asking questions can be interesting,
but, when made an end (as in certain versions of Seeking for Truth as
a higher end than finding truth),[6] becomes perverse and self-defeating.
If you are not seeking an answer, you have not really asked a question.

A bumper sticker proclaims, "To Question Is the Answer." I
question that answer.

To realize ends well is to thrive. Thriving requires striving — trying,
trying hard. Striving requires the virtues.

Can one prove — argue strongly for — the reality and importance
of value? That question is much debated. This book has taken a stand.
I think one can so argue, partly because philosophers do argue strongly
for the reality and importance of the virtues. For instance, Peter Geach,
who argues as follows:

> Virtues [specifically, the cardinal virtues] are needed for any large-
> scale worthy enterprise, just as health and sanity are needed. We
> need prudence or practical wisdom for any large-scale planning. We
> need justice to secure cooperation and mutual trust among men
> . . . . We need temperance in order not to be deflected from our
> long-term . . . goals . . . . And we need courage in order to persevere
> in face of setbacks, weariness, difficulties, and dangers.[7]

We need the virtues because we must make choices, and because
choices can go wrong. Prudence — good sense, good judgment — is
needed to keep choices from going wrong.

The world is very open and very stubborn. Many, many choices
exist; most of the possible ones are wrong. One can drive to New
Orleans from St. Petersburg in many ways, in infinite ways if one
counts as different each possibility of a stop at a motel, or service
station, or gift shop, or landscape, or if one counts brief side visits
along the way. Some ways cease to be driving to New Orleans. To say,
"I'm driving to New Orleans from St. Petersburg via San Francisco"
is to make a joke, even if the itinerary is correct. But, while the ways

of driving to New Orleans from St. Petersburg are unlimited, a much much greater number of routes will fail to get there. And to drive to New Orleans from St. Petersburg, all the logistics need to get done. One cannot skip a mile or leave the steering wheel behind. The world is very open and very stubborn. To artists as well as scientists, to poets as well as scholars.

Possibilities are real, and can be developed or frustrated. Only acorns can become oaks. Most acorns do not become oaks. We can go wrong. In the physical realm, crippling, pain, death. In the social realm, confusion, discord. In the intellectual realm, error. In the moral realm, sin. In the artistic realm, the unformed, the unmoored, fantasy not achieving a just and lively image of reality.

The world is very open and very stubborn. Our task is to make the best moves we can, in hope and faith, in freedom and limit. To care. To reflect. To try. To try to understand.

People are people, and therefore should be treated as people. That's an argument. Treat people as people *because* they are people. That's also one way of putting the Golden Rule ("as ye would that men should do to you, do ye also to them likewise") and the second half of the Summary of the Law ("Thou shalt love thy neighbour as thyself").

That truth is not all sweetness and light. People are people, so check the locks on your doors. People are people, so sanctions are needed, and requirements, structures, deadlines, demands. People are people, so courage and temperance and self-control are requisites for dealing with people.

People are people, and therefore should be treated as people. That truth has a positive side, too. People are people and therefore cannot (not only 'should not' but 'cannot') be treated otherwise. If one tries to treat them without concern, purely as means to one's own ends, one violates them, and will offend them unless the hypocrisy is very skillful, and violates oneself, one's nature, one's humanity. Courtesy is the primary requirement of justice, not particular forms of courtesy, which vary, but the fundamental courtesy of respecting people as people, recognizing that they are capable of learning, virtue, and piety, and capable also of being hurt, being frustrated, being badly cut loose.

Good judgment, wisdom, in any discipline takes years of practice, reflection, learning to judge. To judge literature well takes thought, analysis, precepts, responsiveness, wide reading and experience. Good poetry requires learning, caring, passion, imagination, faith, reflection, and discipline.

The concept of goodness is a difficult, much-argued, hard-to-analyze concept, which is worth long reflection. To be good is hard, a long struggle with tendencies and dispositions and confusions in the soul. And yet we all know people — often people of little book-learning — who are good and who make what is good flourish about them. My poem "Learning Goodness" is a dialogue, really an interior dialogue, about such matters. With it I shall end this book.

Learning Goodness

"Slow the preparation,
Slow the grasping
of the concept
of the good."

"As simple as the touching of a hand.
As simple as the meaning of 'Obey'."

"Are we in disagreement?"

"Not at all.
Reflect, and obey."[8]

NOTES

CHAPTER 1

1. The question was suggested to me by the title of Wolfgang Kohler's *The Place of Value in a World of Fact* (New York: Liveright, 1938). Kohler himself explicitly opposes "Positivism" (p. vii) and "Monism" (pp. 411 — 413), seeks to justify and explain value ("requiredness," p. 72 et passim), and denies that the world of facts is the world: "nature reveals the same dualism between mere facts and selective tendencies as that which characterizes mental life" (p. 411). Nor does the title strictly imply that the world consists of facts only. The world of facts could be a world, as we might say, without denying the existence of computers, 'the place of computers in the business world'. But the empiricistic positivistic pressure is nonetheless strong in the phrase (and in the book), suggesting that the world of facts is the real world or at least a metaphysically-and epistemologically-privileged world.

2. One might reply, 'The illusion is a fact'. To admit that much is to admit into the world of fact psychological fact (the act of erring), conceptual fact, and at least one evaluation as fact — the evaluation of the illusion as a mistake. Which is to admit value as fact.

    It would be all right if "fact" were just used innocently as "a truth" or "a reality to which a truth refers." But the use of "fact" isn't innocent; it's warped by its empirical-positivist history, and that would be more or less all right (though a proponent couldn't say "all right" or be a *pro*ponent, since to say or be so would involve value) if proponents stuck to "fact" as hard-physical-verifiable-facts. But they don't. Its the tergiversation and secret torsion which need exposing.

3. In class lectures at the University of California, Berkeley, according to Dana Smith, one of Professor Bundy's students.

4. Karl Pearson, *The Grammar of Science* (London: Adam and Charles Black, 1911), p. 12.

5. Professor Maynard Metcalf testifying in court at the trial of John T. Scopes in Dayton, Tennessee (the "evolution trial), as quoted by Richard Weaver, *The Ethics of Rhetoric* (Chicago: Henry Regnery Co., 1953), p. 43. Weaver is quoting from *The World's Most Famous Court Trial* (Cincinatti: National Book Co., 1925), a complete transcript, in this and other Scopes-trial quotations.

6. Wilbur A. Nelson, Scopes trial, as quoted by Weaver, *Rhetoric*, p. 42.

7. Charles H. Judd, Scopes trial, quoted by Weaver, *Rhetoric*, pp. 41 — 42.

8. Jacob G. Lipman, Scopes trial, quoted by Weaver, *Rhetoric*, p. 42.

9. Weaver, *Rhetoric*, p. 91.

10. Owen Barfield, *The Rediscovery of Meaning and Other Essays* (Middletown, CT: Wesleyan University Press, 1977), p. 137.

11. E.g., Louis O. Katsoff, *Logic and the Nature of Reality*, 2nd ed. (The Hague, Netherlands: Martinus Nijhoff, 1967), esp. pp. 126 — 127, or the following striking sentence: "For if the doubt [about an accepted fact] were not a reasonable one then the *fact* that it existed would not be evidence that that which had been accepted as a *fact* was not a *fact*" (italics mine), in Norman Malcolm, "The Verification Argument," in *Philosophical Analysis*, ed. Max Black, 1950 (Reprint ed., Freeport, NY: Books for Libraries Press, 1971), p. 241. Cf. Friedrich Waismann, "Verifiability," in *Logic and Language, First Series*, ed. Antony Flew (Oxford: Basil Blackwell, 1951), pp. 136 — 137.

"There is a group of words such as "fact"; "event"; "situation" . . . which
. . . serve as pegs: it's marvellous what a lot of things you can put on them
("the fact that --"). So far they are very handy; but as soon as one focuses on
them and asks, e.g. "What *is* a fact?" they betray a tendency of melting away"
(italics in text).

12.   P. F. Strawson, "Truth. II," in *Aristotelian Society Proceedings (1950)*,
      Supplementary Volume 24, p. 136.

13.   Ludwig Wittgenstein, *Tractatus-Logico-Philosophicus*, trans. D. F. Pears and B.
      F. McGuiness, intro. by Bertrand Russell. German and English texts. (New
      York: Humanities Press; London: Routledge and Kegan Paul, 1961), section
      1.1, p. 7. Cf. section 2.0121, p. 49: "The totality of true propositions is the
      whole of natural science (or the whole corpus of natural sciences)." Wittgenstein
      was not content with the *Tractatus*'s reduction and went beyond it. The influence
      of the *Tractatus*, however, has been one force for the identification of *Tatsachen*
      (facts) with natural science and natural science alone, although "fact" is used
      even in the *Tractatus* in other ways. (Cf. the next note and the quotation it
      refers to in the text.)

14.   Ibid., section 2.0131. p 9.

15.   Gottlob Frege, *Begriffschrifft: A Formula Language, Modeled upon that of Arithmetic,
      For Pure Thought*, in *Frege and Godel*, ed. Jean von Heijenoort (Cambridge,
      MA: Harvard University Press, 1970), pp. 12 — 13, sect. 3. For German text,
      see Gottlob Frege, *Begriffschrift and Andere Aufsätze* (1879; reprint ed., Hildsheim,
      Germany: George Olms 1964), pp.3 — 4. The German word translated *fact*
      is *Thatsache*.

16.   E.g., "Moral facts" are discussed by A. E. Taylor, in *Does God Exist?* (London:
      Macmillan and Co. 1948), pp. 84, 85. In the context, esp. pp. 82 — 85, he is
      arguing that moral truth is as much truth as scientific truth: "All *fact* has a
      right to be taken into account, not only those facts, or aspects of facts, with
      which some department of science is specially concerned," p.83 (italics in text).
      The word *fact* has trouble escaping its scientific and historical shackles, even
      when an argument such as Taylor's *should* set it free.

17.   Charles Darwin, *The Descent of Man*, 2nd ed. (New York: Hurst and Co., 1874),
      p. 630.

18.   Dwight D. Murphy, "Myths and American Constitutional History," in
      Intercollegiate Review, 14 (Fall 1978, no. 1): 14.

19.   R. G. Collingwood, *An Essay on Metaphysics* (Oxford: Clarendon Press, 1940),
      p. 145 (italics mine).

20.   Cf. Paul Holmer, *The Grammar of Faith* (San Francisco: Harper and Row,
      1978), p. 106, "We treat the word *fact* as if it were self-explanatory and
      ground-level, as if there were essential features of everything, open to inspection,
      lying under it" (italics in text); and Stephen Toulmin, *The Philosophy of Science*
      (London: Hutchinson University Library, 1953), p. 115, "To talk . . . of
      theoretical physics falsifying by abstraction, and to ask for the facts and nothing
      but the facts, is to demand the impossible, like asking for a map drawn to no
      particular projection and having no particular scale."

21.   Margaret MacDonald, "Ethics and the Ceremonial Use of Language," in
      Analysis. ed. Black, p. 201.

22.   Thomas Hobbes, *Leviathan*, in *The English Works of Thomas Hobbes*, ed. William
      Molesworth, 11 vols, 1839 for vol. 3; Reprint ed. (Aalen, Germany: Scientia
      Verlag. 1966), 3: 143 (italics in text).

23.   Walter Scott, "Personality Parade,"in *Parade*, May 20, 1979, inside of front
      cover, Chattanooga *Times*, May 20, 1979.

24.   Advertisement for Pacific Research.

25.   " Health: Facts and Fallacies," in *Family Weekly*, (Chattanooga *News-Free Press*,
      Sunday, May 4, 1980), p. 29.

26. Advertisement for *The New Columbia Encyclopedia*, quoting *The New York Times Book Review*.

27. Weaver, *Rhetoric*, p. 30.

28. Kirkley F. Mather, Scopes trial, quoted by Weaver, *Rhetoric*, p. 43.

29. Charlton Hinman, *Printing and Proofreading of the First Folio of Shakespeare*, 2 vols. (Oxford: Clarendon Press, 1963), 1: 50 (italics in text).

30. Stephen Toulmin and June Goodfield, *The Discovery of Time* (New York: Harper and Row, 1965), pp. 271 — 272.

31. Owen, *Rediscovery*, p. 178.

32. Herbert Feigl, "De Principiis Non Disputandum . . . ? [spaced periods in text]: On the Meaning and Limits of Justification," in *Analysis*, ed. Max Black (1950), p. 114.

33. Feigl, Ibid., p. 133.

34. Richard D. Altick, *Victorian Studies in Scarlet* (New York: W. W. Norton and Co., 1970), pp. 230 — 231.

35. Sir Arthur Conan Doyle, "The Sign of Four," in *The Complete Sherlock Holmes*, preface by Christopher Morley (Garden City, NY: Doubleday and Co., [n.d.]), p. 90.

36. Peter Herbst writes in his essay, "The Nature of Facts," in *Essays in Conceptual Analysis*, ed. Antony Flew (New York: St. Martin's Press; London: Macmillan and Co., 1966), p. 156, "My procedure has roughly been to investigate what sort of things are *properly* called facts" (italics mine). Properly so, since he wishes his essay to be of value.

37. Hyder Edward Rollins, "Appendix X: The Rival Poet" in William Shakespeare, *The Sonnets*, ed. Hyder Edward Rollins. Variorum Edition of Shakespeare (Philadelphia and London: J. P. Lippincott Co., 1944), 2: 294.

38. Ibid., 2: 43. Paul Ramsey, *The Fickle Glass: A Study of Shakespeare's Sonnets* (New York: AMS Press, 1979), pp. 5 — 7, offers argument to establish Shakespeare's authorship.

39. Ibid., 2: 55.

40. Ibid., 2: 73.

41. Fredson Bowers writes, in *On Editing Shakespeare* (Charlottesville, VA: University Press of Virginia, 1966), p. 5, "If every *possible fact* were known about a text, an editor's judgment would be subject to much less strain [actually it would make editorial labors very, very much lengthier — at least now we can guess, some]. But invariably the case is not only that *unrecognized facts* are present though overlooked, not only that *presumed facts* are subject to misinterpretation, but also that in the nature of the problem all the *necessary facts* can never be determined on the basis of the preserved documents" (italics mine). Are non-presumed facts not subject to misinterpretation?

42. Peter Geach, *The Virtues* (Cambridge and New York: Cambridge University Press, 1977), p. 14.

43. Rollins, *Sonnets*, 2: 53.

44. Ibid., 2: 53 — 54.

45. Ibid., 2: 54 — 55.

46. Samuel Schoenbaum, *Shakespeare's Lives* (New York: Oxford University Press; Oxford: Clarendon Press, 1970), p. 747.

47. Ibid., p. 746.

48. Cf. Peter Geach's discussion of Plato's *Euthyphro*, in Geach's *Logic Matters* (Berkeley and Los Angeles: University of California Press, 1972), pp. 35 — 37.

49. J. A. Montgomery, "The New Sources of Knowledge," in *Record and Revelation*, ed. Henry Wheeler Robinson (Oxford: Clarendon Press, 1938), p. 24.

50. Cf. Herbst, "Facts," p. 151, "*That which entitles us to say that a statement is true*

and that which entitles us to say that a . . . *statement states a fact, are one and the same"* (italics in text).

51.   The impulse to reduce all to fact (or events or whatever) can lead at times to a wild sort of multi-pluralism, a world (if one can call it that) of lots and lots and lots of facts or events or whatevers, separate and disconnected. E.g., Bertrand Russell, *Philosophy* (New York: W. W. Norton and Co., 1927), pp. 271 — 282, (italics in text), develops a "monism" in which the world is made out of "only one *kind* of stuff, namely events" (p. 282), but a "pluralism in the sense that it [the monism] admits the existence of a great multiplicity of events, each minimal event being a logically self-subsistent entity" (p. 282). If the entities are connected, related, the monism vanishes, since there would then be both events and relations. (If one denies that relations are entities, one is still left with a 1+–ism instead of monism, since relations surely aren't *nothing*.)

52.   Russell, Ibid., p.7, who ascribes the theory to Edmund Gosse's father. Russell states that Gosse held that "fossils . . . [were] inserted [by God] to try our faith," (p. 7), which Gosse does not say. See Philip Henry Gosse, *Omphalos* (London; John Van Voorst, 1857) esp. pp. 346 — 347.
      Gosse's basic arguments are to be found on pp. vi — viii, 110 — 126, 335 — 372. Gosse (who relates that he is not the originator of the basic view — see p. vi and vii) argues that each kind of physical organism has a circular existence (for instance, p. 116, flower-carpel-legume-seed-cotyledons-shoot-stem-bud-flower-and so on) and consequently that an organism newly created by God at any point of the organism's development would necessarily bear marks of the past within it. Therefore a scientist (available *ex hypothesi* on the First day of Creation) who tried to judge the age of an organism would give an answer right by his method. For instance (pp. 127 — 134) he would give at least thirty years as the minimum age of a mature tree-fern, when actually the tree-fern would be less than one day old. The thirty years are prechronic — existent as-if in God's mind but not in the time of the actual creation. [One might comment that, if those prechronic years existed in God's mind, it would be in some real sense real, and, since (or if) God would be,'before' the Creation, the only awareness, the difference between prechronic and 'actual' time would be strangely elusive-to-vanishing.]
      Gosse is fair-minded, claims only to have reached a possibility of reconcilement of the testimony of the rocks and the testimony of Scripture, recognizes and discusses interestingly the difference (or apparent difference) between the nonorganic and organic, and makes in my judgement a real philosophic and poetic contribution in his recognition and exploration of the notion of the past-as-contained-in-the-present. He deserved better treatment than he got.
      See Edmund Gosse, *Father and Son*, new ed. (London: William Heinemann, 1928), pp. 107 — 109, who tells us that the scornful laughter at Philip Gosse's attempted mediation was loud, the consequent suffering real. "My Father used to tramp in solitude round and round the red ploughed field which was going to be his lawn, or, sheltering himself from the thin Devonian rain, pace up and down the still naked verandah" (p. 111).
      Philosophers are people.

53.   Cf. George Depue Hadzsits, *Lucretius and His Influence*, (New York: Longmans, Green and Co., 1935), esp. pp. 70 — 72.

54.   Cf. Lucretius, *De Rerum Natura*, ed. Williams Ellery Leonard and Stanley Barney Smith (Madison, WI, and London: University of Wisconsin Press, 1968), respectively Book 1, vv. 330 — 334, p. 238; Book 2, vv. 333-336, p. 343; Book 2, vv. 61 — 66, p. 318; Book 2, vv. 215 — 222, p. 334; Book 1, vv. 370 — 383, pp. 241 — 242; Book 1, vv. 459 — 482, pp. 249 — 251. For an English version, see *Lucretius on the Nature of Things*, trans. Cyril Bailey (Oxford: Clarendon Press, 1910), respectively pp. 38, 76, 67, 73, 39, and 42.

55. Cf. Lucretius, *Natura*, ed. Leonard, Book 3. vv. 176 — 226, pp. 438 — 442 (the nature of the soul); Book 6 vv. 1 — 95, pp. 769 — 777 (for the gods). Cf. Lucretius, *Nature*, trans. Bailey, respectively, pp. 112 — 113, 235 — 238.

56. Parmenides, *Parmenides*, ed. Leonardo Taran (Princeton: Princeton University Press, 1965), text, esp. Fragment 8, vv. 1 — 61, pp. 82 — 86, and commentary, esp. pp. 191 — 201.

57. Cf. G. J. Warnock, *English Philosophy since 1900* (London and New York: Oxford University Press, 1958), pp. 36 — 37; and Renford Bambrough, *Reason, Truth, and God* (London: Methuen & Co., 1969), pp. 56 — 57.

For a summary of some resistance to the factualists, see Appendix B, "Two-Score and More Witnesses against the Fact-Value Split," in Wayne C. Booth's *Modern Dogma and the Rhetoric of Assent* (Chicago and London: University of Chicago Press, 1974, paper), pp. 207 — 211.

CHAPTER 2

1. David Hume, *A Treatise of Human Nature*, ed. L. A. Selby-Bigge (Oxford: Clarendon Press, 1888), p. 458.

2. Ibid., p. 457 (italics in text).

3. Ibid., p. 458.

4. Ibid., p. 463.

5. Ibid., pp. 268 — 269 (italics in text). Hume parallels this argument closely in *Enquiries concerning Human Understanding and concerning the Principles of Morals*, ed. L. A. Selby-Bigge. Third ed., with text revised and notes by P. H. Nidditch (Oxford: Clarendon Press, 1975), pp. 287 — 289.

6. Genesis 3.5, King James version.

7. Cf. Ludwig Wittgenstein, *On Certainty*, ed. G. E. M. Anscombe and G. H. von Wright, trans. Denis Paul and G. E. M. Anscombe, German and English Texts (New York and Evanston: Harper and Row, J. J. Harper Editions, 1969), section 557, p. 73e [English]; "the language-game is so to say something unpredictable. I mean: it is not based on grounds. It is not reasonable (or unreasonable).
   It is there — like our life."
   In our life and language we must judge and evaluate and decide. We encounter value.

8. William Butler Yeats, *A Vision* (New York: Macmillan Co., Collier Books, 1966), p. 25, "to hold in a single thought reality and justice." Cf. Allen Tate, *The Forlorn Demon* (Chicago: Henry Regnery Co., 1953), p. 29.

9. David Hume, *The Life of David Hume, Esq. Written by Himself* (London: W. Strahan and T. Cadell, 1777), pp. 32 — 35 (italics mine).

CHAPTER 3

1. Wittgenstein, *Certainty*, section 482, p. 63e [English], "It is as if 'I know' did not tolerate a metaphysical emphasis." Cf. esp. section 11, p. 3 [German] and p. 3e [English]; section 24, pp. 5 and 5e; section 347, pp. 44 and 44e; section 407, pp. 52 and 52e; section 467, pp. 61 and 61e.

2. Cf. Aristotle, *Posterior Analytics*, trans. Jonathan Barnes (Oxford: Clarendon

Press, 1975), esp. pp. 2 — 3 (Book 1, Chapter 2, 71b: 18 — 25) and p. 5
(Book 1, Chapter 2, 72b: 19 — 26). For Greek text see Aristotle's *Prior and
Posterior Analytics*, ed. W. D. Ross (Oxford: Clarendon Press, 1949), 71a: 16
— 25 and 72b: 18 — 25 [Greek text is not explicitly paginated]. Aristotle
holds that there is, in having true knowledge, both demonstration (valid
syllogistic deduction) and "also some principles of understanding by which we
become familiar with the definitions [non-demonstrable premises]," p. 5 (Book
1, Chapter 3, 72b: 26 — 27). Cf. Antony Kenny, *The Anatomy of the Soul*
(Oxford: Basil Blackwell, 1973), p. 33, who calls the non-demonstrable premises
"self-evident principles."
Suppose some supposings.
Suppose one grants Aristotle's view, including the full-knowability of the non-
demonstrable premises. Then for a given case when one had correctly argued,
one would have established, with absolute rational certainty the conclusion.
But suppose one had doubts about one's own reasoning (sensible or not —
maybe just the thought "I may have made some mistake") would then one
have the absolute certainty? Can one *have* absolute rational certainty and *doubt*
whether one has? (I'm not sure.)
Suppose that one grants Aristotle's view and denies that we can know non-
demonstrable premises with absolute certainty; then one would conclude that
we cannot have knowledge in that full sense. One would have firmly established
a mild form of scepticism.
Suppose then one learned that modern philosophers often scorn Book 1 of
the *Posterior Analytics* (see Barnes, "Introduction," p. ix). For example, G. E.
M. Anscombe, in *Three Philosophers* (Ithaca: Cornell University Press, 1961),
p. 6, calls Book 1 of the *Posterior Analytics* Aristotle's "worst book." Suppose,
consequently, rationally or not, one's trust in the firmly-established scepticism
was shaken. Then, one would think, "Gee, I don't know; maybe we can achieve
absolute certainty." And then one might read Barnes's defense of Aristotle
against such critics (p. ix — xiii) and have doubts about those doubts.
Putting Aristotle by, can we be really certain that we don't ever have absolute
rational certainty, unless we have established with absolute rational certainty
that we cannot? But if we had done that self-inconsistent feat, it would be false
(and true — and since false and true — false) that we had established we
cannot ever have absolute rational certainty.
We do have certainty, firm and founded belief we call knowledge. As for
knowledge, God has *knowledge*. And we?
Something hauntingly near is yet to say.
3.   The line alluded to, very much and deliberately reapplied, is from Emerson's
      poem "Brahma" (stanza 3, line 2) in *Poems*, vol. 9 of *The Complete Works of
      Ralph Waldo Emerson* (1903-1904, 1904 for vol. 9); 2nd ed. of reprint edition
      (New York: AMS Press, Inc., 1979), p. 195.
4.   Cf. Wittgenstein, *Certainty*, section 450, p. 59e, "a doubt that doubted
      everything would not be a doubt."
5.   Cf. my discussion of Wallace Stevens in *The Lively and the Just* (Tuscaloosa:
      University of Alabama Press, 1962), pp. 103 — 117, esp. p. 116.
6.   I am not denying that there is a fascination in beginnings, and some puzzles.
      E.g., Georg W. F. Hegel, *Hegel's Science of Logic*, trans. W. H. Johnston and L.
      G. Struthers, 2 vol. (New York: Macmillan Co.; London: George Allen and
      Unwin, 1929), 1:85 — 87, and context. For German text see Georg Wilhelm
      Friedrich Hegel, *Wissenschaft der Logik*, ed. Georg Lasson, 2 vols. (1932; reprint
      ed., Hamburg, Germany: Felix Meiner, 1971), 1:58 — 60 and context.
      "So far, there is Nothing; Something is to become. The Beginning is not pure
      Nothing, but a Nothing from which Something is to proceed; so that Being is
      already contained in the Beginning. The Beginning thus contains both, Being

and Nothing" (1:85; German text, 1:58), and "But the beginning must not be a first *and* an other; in a thing which in itself is first *and* an other, progress has already advanced a step" (1:87, italics in text; German text, 1:60, no italics in text).

Edges are odd, neither air nor bridge; and beginning is a most-special sort of (almost) edge. But meanwhile, there are things to realize and form, decisions to decide, jobs to get done.

7. See Alan Ryan, *The Philosophy of the Social Sciences* (New York: Pantheon Books, 1970), p. 143, "to have no artistic appreciation makes it not merely more difficult to write the history of art; it renders it *logically impossible*, because it means that the proffered account cannot be a history of art *as* art" [italics in text].

8. G. E. Moore, "Proof of an External World,"in *Philosophical Papers* (New York: Crowell-Collier Publishing Co., Collier Books, 1962), pp. 126 — 148, p. 144 for the quotation. I did not think, so far as I can remember, of the Moore argument when I wrote, in the summer of 1964, the first version of the Homer-value argument, but I had read the Moore argument earlier and heard it discussed by Renford Bambrough, when, on a visit to the University of the Pacific in November 1962, he offered an argument for moral knowledge specifically based on the Moore argument. Bambrough's argument is repeated in Bambrough's *Moral Scepticism and Moral Knowledge* (London: Routledge and Kegan Paul, 1970), p. 15 and context.

9. I have in mind particularly the themes (and styles) of Jacques Derrida and the style (and themes) of Roland Barthes. E.g., Jacques Derrida, "Cogito and the History of Madness," in *Writing and Difference*, trans. Alan Bass (Chicago: University of Chicago Press, 1978), p. 62. For French text, see *L'écriture et la différence* ([Paris]: Editions du Seuil, 1967), pp. 95 — 96. Derrida is approvingly discussing and in some part paraphrasing Michel Foucault.

"The relationship between reason, madness, and death is . . . a structure of deferral whose irreducible originality must be respected. The attempt-to-say-the-demoniac hyperbole is not an attempt among others [but very basic and praiseworthy] . . . . But this crisis in which reason is madder than madness [since madness is nearer to basic reality] . . . this crisis has always begun and is interminable." One cannot really coherently *say* any of that (as Derrida knows or adumbrates), because, since the ultimate, primordial reality is demonic, and language incompetent, language can never truly evaluate the relation of anything to reality, including and especially (and interminably) language. Of course one cannot say *that*, either, or *that*, and so on and so regressively under and about.

But what if the demonic is only deadly and strong, but not ultimate? Then we can use language well, and act in good hope (as well as in fear).

For Barthes' style, open at random. The following is fairly central of theme as well as twisty enough of style: *The Pleasure of the Text*, trans. Richard Miller (New York: Hill and Wang, 1975), p. 65 (italics in text). For French text see *Le Plaisir du Texte* (Paris: Éditions du Seuil, 1973), pp. 102 — 103.

"Pleasure's force of *suspension* [and Barthes is choosing pleasure as destructive of morality and truth — in his immediately preceding paragraph] can never be overstated: it is . . . a stoppage which congeals all recognized values (recognized by oneself). Pleasure is a *neuter* (the most perverse form of the demoniac).

Or, at least, what pleasure suspends is the *signified* value: the (good) cause."

I agree that pleasure in reading includes powerful and appropriate response to just evaluation (which Barthes, shortly before, admitted) and that pleasure in reading is not only the pleasure of powerfully appropriate response to just evaluation. For instance, we can have the pleasure of powerfully appropriate response to beauty of structure, or pleasantly appropriate response to ingenuity of wit; and pleasure is not wholly analyzable or reducible to response *qua* response. But that does *not* mean that the other pleasures are inconsistent with just evaluation or need be perversely imposed on the text. I agree that treating the immoral as the a-moral is a form of the demonic; to call it the most perverse form of the demonic is a curious hyperbole.

10.   C. S. Lewis, *The Abolition of Man* (New York: Crowell-Collier Publishing Co., Collier Books, 1962), p. 95. He goes on to say, "For those who do not perceive its rationality, even universal consent could not prove it" (which is true). The notion of "perceiving its rationality" is very close to the notion of proof. Not everything in a system can be severally proved within the system without circularity; but that is a different issue, and certainly does not prove as such that moral precepts or principles are purely-intuited axioms.

CHAPTER 4

1.   Longinus', *On the Sublime*, trans. W. Hamilton Fyfe, in Aristotle *The Poetics*; 'Longinus', *On the Sublime*; Demetrius, *On Style*. The Loeb Classical Library (London: William Heinemann; Cambridge: Harvard University Press, 1965), section 6, p. 137.

2.   Aristotle, *The Poetics*, trans. W. Hamilton Fyfe, in Ibid., section 13, pp. 45 — 47.

3.   Matthew 22.40, King James version.

4.   John Dryden, "A Defence of an Essay of Dramatic Poesy," in *Of Dramatic Poesy and Other Critical Essays*, ed. George Watson, 2 vols. Everyman's Library (New York: E. P. Dutton; London: J. M. Dent and Sons, 1962), 1: 122.

5.   Dryden, "Of Dramatic Poesy," Ibid., 1: 22 (italics in text).

6.   Paul Ramsey *The Art of John Dryden* (Lexington: University of Kentucky Press, 1969), esp. pp. 175 — 177, 179 — 180, and Hoyt Trowbridge, "The Place of the Rules in Dryden's Criticism," in *Modern Philology*, 44 (1946): 84 — 96.

7.   Paul Ramsey *The Lively and the Just* (Tuscaloosa: University of Alabama Press, 1962), pp. 139 — 140, and "Nature in Criticism" in "Nature," in *Encyclopedia of Poetry and Poetics*, ed. Alex Preminger (Princeton: Princeton University Press, 1965), p. 555.

8.   Thomas Hobbes, *Leviathan*, in *The English Works of Thomas Hobbes*, ed. William Molesworth, 11 vols., 1839 for vol. 3 (Reprint ed.; Aalen, W. Germany: Scientia Verlag, 1966), 3: 258.

9.   Ibid., 3. 262.

10.   See Bertrand Russell, *Philosophy* (New York: W. W. Norton and Co., 1927), p. 225, "Everyone admits that you should lie if you meet a homicidial maniac pursuing a man with a view to murdering him."

11.   Peter Geach, *The Virtues* (Cambridge and New York: Cambridge University Press, 1977), p. 121.

12.   To-say-the-thing-which-is-not is the great name for lying given in the Fourth Voyage of Jonathan Swift's *Gulliver's Travels 1726*, ed. Herbert Davis. Intro. by Harold Williams. Rev. Edition. The Prose Works of Jonathan Swift (Oxford: Basil Blackwell, 1959), p. 240. The hyphenation of the phrase is mine.

13.   Ludwig Wittgenstein, *On Certainty*, ed. G. E. M. Anscombe, and G. H. von Wright, trans. Denis Paul and G. E. M. Anscombe, German and English Texts (New York and Evanston: Harper and Row, J. J. Harper Editions, 1969), section 248, p. 33e [English].

14. Alexander Pope, "Epilogue to the Satires, Dialogue II," vv. 208 — 209, in *Imitations of Horace*, ed. John Butt, 2nd ed. Vol. 4 of the Twickenham Edition (New Haven: Yale University Press; London: Methuen and Co., 1953), p. 324.

CHAPTER 5

1. Cf. George Connor, "A Minor Virtue,"in *Hints and Guesses* (Chattanooga: St. Peter's Episcopal Church, 1982), (Cincinnati: Forward Movement Publications, forthcoming.) p. 86, esp. paragraph 2.
2. Hammurabi, *The Code of Hammurabi of Babylon about 2250 B.C.*, ed. and trans. Robert Francis Harper, Transliteration of the Babylonian Text and an English translation (Chicago: The University of Chicago Press, 1904), nos. 53 and 54, pp. 29 — 31 (English).
3. "Prologue" Ibid., p. 9 (English).
4. Elbert L. Little, *The Audubon Society Field Guide to North American Trees: Eastern Region* (New York: Alfred A. Knopf, 1980), p. 282.
5. Cf. Plato, *Theaeteus*, 170A — 171 in *Theaeteus and Sophist*, ed. Harold North Fowler. *Plato*, vol. 2, The Loeb Classical Library. (Cambridge: Harvard University Press; London: William Heinemann, 1942), pp. 106 — 113.
6. Lucretius, *De Rerum Natura*, ed. William Ellery Leonard and Stanley Barney Smith (Madison and London: University of Wisconsin Press, 1968), Book 2, vv. 225 — 235, p. 334. Cf. *Lucretius on the Nature of Things*, trans. Cyril Bailey (Oxford: Clarendon Press, 1910), p. 73.
7. Emile Durkheim uses the term *anomie* (since become a commonplace) and related terms recurrently, e.g. Chapter One entitled, "The Anomic Division of Labor" in *Emile Durkheim on the Division of Labor in Society*, ed. George Simpson (New York: Macmillan Co., 1933), pp. 353 — 373. For French text see Emile Durkheim, *De La Division du Travail Social*, 2nd ed. (Paris: Félix Alcan, 1902), pp. 343 — 365 (Book 3, Chap. 1, "La Division du Travail Anomique"). Cf. for interpretation and further references, Ralph Bertram Ginsberg, *Anomie and Aspiration* (New York: Arno Press, 1980), esp. Footnotes, Chap. 1, pp. 15 — 20, and Bibliography, pp. 317 — 328.
8. Homer, *The Odyssey*, trans. Robert Fitzgerald (Garden City, NY: Doubleday and Co., 1963), Book Fourteen, p. 254. Cf., for Greek text, Homer, *The Odyssey*, trans. A. T. Murray, The Loeb Classical Library (London: William Heinemann; Cambridge: Harvard University Press, 1919), p. 50, vv. 227 — 228.
9. E.g., Bertrand Russell, "The Recrudescence of Puritanism," in *Sceptical Essays* (New York: W. W. Norton and Co., 1928), pp. 124 — 131 (italics mine in what follows except as noted).
    Russell states (p. 124) "a man or woman *ought* to be free in regard to enjoyments which do not damage other people" (intended as a general moral truth).
    He states (p. 127) "the suppression of a *real evil*, if carried out too drastically, produces other *evils* which are even greater." That is, there are real evils, some worse than others, as is also clearly implicit in the following (p. 130): "love of power does far more *harm* than love of drink."
    He states (p. 131) that "life cannot remain tolerable unless we learn to let each other alone in all matters that are not of immediate and obvious concern of the community." That is, there are valid social ends, some actions *should be* controlled for the common good, other actions *should* not be controlled. The context makes it clear that he is speaking of the whole world. That is, there is cross-cultural moral truth.

He also states (p. 128) "The *real evil* here [in the "white-slave traffic" (p. 128)] is very grave, and quite a proper matter for the criminal law." That is, there are real evils which should be subject to criminal law.

He states (p. 131), "We must . . . not . . . impose our moral standards on each other [which should cheer up white-slavers]. The Puritan imagines that his moral standard is *the* moral standard [italics in text]; he does not realize that other ages and other countries, and even groups in his country, have *moral standards* different from his, to which they have as *good* a *right* as he has to his."

Russell has, then, maintained or implied the following views in the essay. There are real moral truths. There are no real moral truths, only differing moral standards. Some moral standards are more important that others and should overrule. All moral standards are equal. Every one has an equal and real right to his unreal moral standards. Societies should impose their standards on those who disagree (in matters of "immediate and obvious concern"). Societies should not impose their standards on others in or out of their societies [the implication of that is that no laws should ever be passed].

The chaos could hardly be more total, yet the essay is skillful and indignant propaganda, with some grains and lumps of truth among the confusion.

Relativism has polemical advantages.

10. We know that there are, in the oceans of the world, flora and fauna yet undiscovered by human beings. Those flora and fauna, which we know to exist, are not part of our experience.

11. Or perhaps the necessity is a *good* proof. Can one have a valid *argument* or *proof* for scepticism or fideism based on the truth that one must use the conditions of argument or proof to argue or prove? Is it a logical mistake to presume that the logical dictum, roughly stated, 'Circular proof does not prove' can be used *against* the bases of logic or our certainty thereof? What meta-levels are under-involved? In any event, I *do* have a faith in the veracity of experience and in the (great but limited) power of logic.

CHAPTER 7

1. Cf. Stephen Toulmin, *The Philosophy of Science* (London: Hutchinson University Library, 1953), speaking (pp. 112 — 116) of Sir Arthur Eddington's question concerning how much our physical theories tell about "things in Nature" (p. 112) and how much is contributed by the theorists: "Reading about this subject, as when reading Kant, one gets the impression that to try to draw the line between our own contribution and that of the facts is in some curious way an impossiblity — rather like trying to chew your own teeth" (p. 115), and goes on to say valuable and sensible things.
    (One can chew his own teeth, a bad habit which, done persistently enough, can lead to heavy dental expenses.)

2. Immanuel Kant, *Critique of Pure Reason*, ed. Norman Kemp Smith (New York: Modern Library, 1958), pp. 41 — 47, For German text see Immanuel Kant, *Kritik der Reinen Vernunft*, ed. Karl Kehrbach. (Leipzig, Germany: Philipp Reclam the younger, n.d.), [Preface by editor dated 1878], pp. 48 — 57. See also C.D. Broad, *Kant*, ed. C. Lewy (New York and Cambridge: Cambridge University Press, 1978), pp. 27 — 50 (esp. pp. 50 — 51) and pp. 84 — 85. See also pp. 16 — 17.

3. Cf. Toulmin, *Science*, pp. 124 — 125, on cloud chambers.

4. Cf. G. J. Warnock in his "Introduction" to George Berkeley, *The Principle of Human Knowledge and Three Dialogues between Hylas and Philonous*, ed. G. J. Warnock (Cleveland and New York: Meridian Books, 1963), esp. pp. 12 — 13, 31 — 32; and Thomas Gilby, *Phoenix and Turtle* (London and New York: Longmans, Green and Co., 1950), p. 5.

CHAPTER 8

1. Marc Belth, "The Differentiating Curriculum: A Humane Approach," *Humanities in the South*, no. 49, Spring 1979, p. 2.
   Belth is describing the view, not approving it.

CHAPTER 9

1. Peter Geach, "Aquinas," in G. E. M. Anscombe and Peter Geach, *Three Philosophers* (Ithaca, NY: Cornell University Press, 1961), p. 82.
2. Some philosophers, on duty, know it too, e.g. S. E. Toulmin and K. Baier in their very good essay "On Describing," in *Philosophy and Ordinary Language*, ed. Charles E. Caton (Urbana: University of Illinois Press, 1963), pp. 194 — 219, which includes the following notable example: "if in a murder trial the foreman delivers the verdict, 'We find the prisoner *Guilty*', the prisoner may protest 'It's not true! I didn't do it!', with perfect logical propriety," p. 217 (italics in text).
3. Thomas Aquinas, *Summa Theologica*, ed. Thomas Gilby, 60 vols. Latin and English texts (Cambridge: Blackfriars, 1960 for vol. 18), la2, question 18, article 1, p. 5 (English), "good and being are convertible terms"; p. 4, "bonum enim et ens convertuntur."
4. William Butler Yeats, "From "Oedipus at Colonus"," which is Section 11 of "A Man Young and Old," in *The Collected Poems of W. B. Yeats* (New York: Macmillan and Co., 1951), p. 223.
5. Arthur N. Prior, in *Logic and the Basis of Ethics* (Oxford: Clarendon Press, 1949), gives several historical examples of such (actual or claimed) reductions to tautology of ethical identifications or relations, e.g. pp. 1 — 2, 8, 97 — 98, 104 — 105.

CHAPTER 11

1. G. E. M. Anscombe, "On Brute Facts," *Analysis*, 18 (1958): pp. 69 — 72, which she offers a summary of in her "Modern Moral Philosophy" in *The Is-Ought Question*, ed. W. D. Hudson (New York: St. Martin's Press, 1969), p. 178.
   One of her examples in the earlier essay ("Brute Facts," pp. 70 — 71, italics in text) is beautifully relevant to denying the is-ought hiatus.
   "A set of events is the ordering and supply of potatoes, and something is a bill, only in the context of our institutions.

Now, if my owing the grocer on this occasion does not consist in any facts mentioned, it seems that we must say one of two things. Either *(a)* to say I owe the grocer is nothing but to say that *some such* facts hold, or (b) to say I owe the grocer adds something non-factual to the statement that some such facts hold.

But . . . , if this is a valid point, it holds equally for the description of a set of events as: the grocer's supplying me with potates. And we should not wish to say either of these things about that.

The grocer supplies me with a quarter of potatoes: that is to say, he (1) brings that amount of potatoes to my house and (2) leaves them there. But not any action of taking a lot of potatoes to my house and leaving them there would be *supplying* me with them."

That is, if evaluation requires something non-factual added to the facts, *so do facts.* That is, facts as facts dissolve. That is, facts are evolutions.

2.   A refutation of the theory that moral concepts are not descriptive is given by Peter Geach in *Logic Matters* (Berkeley and Los Angeles: University of California Press, 1972), pp. 268 — 269 (italics in text):
"The theory that to call a kind of act 'bad' is not to describe but to condemn it is open to . . . objections. Let us consider this piece of moral reasoning:

If doing a thing is bad, getting your little brother to do it is bad.
Tormenting the cat is bad.
Ergo, getting your little brother to torment the cat is bad.

The whole nerve of the reasoning is that 'bad' should mean exactly the same at all four occurrences — should not, for example, shift from an evaluative to a descriptive or conventional or inverted-commas use. But in the major premise the speaker (a father, let us suppose) is certainly not uttering acts of condemnation: one could hardly take him to be condemning just *doing a thing.*"

3.   Ray Lepley, *Verifiability of Value* (New York: Columbia University Press, 1964), p. 4.
4.   Ibid.
5.   Ibid., p. 223.
6.   Ibid., p. 222 (italics mine).
7.   Ibid., p. 223.
8.   Ibid., p. 222, in passage referred to by Note 6, above.
9.   Ibid., p. 224.
10. Ibid., p. 225.
11. Ibid., p. 46 (italics in text).
12. Gottlob Frege, "Frege against the Formalists," trans. Max Black, in *Translations from the Philosophical Writings of Gottlob Frege*, ed. Peter Geach and Max Black (Oxford: Basil Blackwell, 1970), p.188. For German text, see [Gottlob] Frege, *Grundgesetze der Arithmetik.* 1893; reprint ed., Hildesheim, Germany: Georg Olms, 1962), vol. 2 [vols. 1 and 2 are in same book, but separately paginated], no. 92, p. 101.
13. Frege, "A Critical Elucidation of Some Points in E. Schroeder . . . " in *Translations from Frege*, p. 100. For German text, see Gottlob Frege, "Kritische Beleuchtung Einiger Punkte in E. Schröder . . . ," in *Kleine Schriften*, ed. Ignacio Angelelli (Hildesheim, Germany: Georg Olms, 1967), p. 205.
14. Gottlob Frege, *The Basic Laws of Arithmetic*, ed. and trans. Montgomery Furth (Berkeley and Los Angeles: University of California Press, 1964), p. 12. For German text see Frege, *Arithmetik*, vol. 1, "Vorwort", p. xv. Cf. p. 15: "Anyone who has once acknowledged a law of truth has . . . acknowledged a law that

prescribes the way in which one ought to judge, no matter where, or when, or by whom the judgment is made." (German text p. xvii).
Cf. Renford Bambrough, *Moral Scepticism and Moral Knowledge* (London: Routledge and Kegan Paul, 1979), p. 104.

15. Max Black, "The Gap between "Is" and "Should"," in *Is-Ought*, ed. Hudson, p. 102.
16. R. M. Hare, "Descriptivism," in *Is-Ought*, ed. Hudson, p. 246.
17. Ibid., p. 241.
18. J. R. Searle, "How to Derive "Ought" from "Is"," in *Is-Ought*, ed. Hudson, pp. 120 — 134.
19. Ibid., p. 121.
20. Ibid., pp. 130 — 131.
21. Ibid., p. 129.
22. Ibid., p. 128.
23. Ibid., p. 130.
24. I quote from Karl R. Popper, *The Open Society and Its Enemies* 2 vols. 5th ed. (Princeton: Princeton University Press, 1966), 1:61 (italics in text). See Antony Flew, "On Not Deriving "Ought" from "Is"," in *Is-Ought*, ed. Hudson, p. 137.
25. Flew, Ibid., p. 137.
26. J. R. Searle, "Deriving 'Ought' from 'Is': Objections and Replies," in *Is-Ought*, ed. Hudson, p. 270.

CHAPTER 12

1. Ludwig Wittgenstein, esp. in *Philosophical Investigations*, trans. G. E. Anscombe, 3rd ed., German and English text, (New York: Macmillan Co., 1958), esp. sections 65 — 77, pp. 31e — 36e. See this chapter, note 4.
2. Peter Geach, in "Plato's Euthyphro," in *Logic Matters* (Berkeley and Los Angeles: University of California Press, 1972) calls it *"the Socratic fallacy,"* p. 33 (italics in text) and discusses and exemplifies its use in Plato, pp. 33 — 35. For some other valuable discussion of limits of definition, see Renford Bambrough, "Aristotle on Justice," in *New Essays on Plato and Aristotle*, ed. Renford Bambrough (New York: Humanities Press; London: Routledge and Kegan Paul, 1965), pp. 167 — 168; John Wisdom, "The Logic of God," in *Paradox and Discovery* (Berkeley and Los Angeles: University of California, 1970), pp. 8 — 9; and F. Waismann, "Analytic-Synthetic," in his *How I See Philosophy*, ed. R. Harré (New York: St. Martin's Press; London: Macmillan and Co., 1968), esp. pp. 140 — 141.
   The assumption that we should begin with clear definition of the 'basic' terms leads to many a mischief and confusion in literary criticism, and to unnecessary scepticism.
   What is literature? a text? a reader? a beginning? a literary work of art? What is a what? for how long in how-long discussion? We discuss, interpret, compare evaluate, talk sense and truth about literary works better than literary theorists can define, and the definings are not needed for the job.
3. Cf. Gottlob Frege, "Thoughts," *Logical Investigations*, ed. Peter Geach, trans. Peter Geach and R. H. Stoothoff (New Haven: Yale University Press, 1977), pp. 2 — 4. For German text, see Gottlob Frege, "Der Gedanke," in *Logische untersuchungen* in *Kleine Schriften*, ed. Ignacio Angelelli (Hildesheim, Germany: Georg Olms, 1967), pp. 343 — 354.

Also compare J. McT. Ellis McTaggart, in *Philosophical Studies*, ed. S. V. Keeling (1934); Reprint ed. (Freeport, NY: Books for Libraries Press, 1966), p. 126: "It is impossible to explain . . . goodness or truth unless by bringing in the term to be explained as part of the explanation, and we thereby reject the explanation as invalid. But we do not therefore reject the notion as erroneous, but accept it as something ultimate, which while it does not admit of explanation, does not require it."

4. Is the use of *good* (*value*) univocal, equivocal, analogical, overlapping, systematically (or partly-systematically) ambiguous, family-resemblancish-in-the-language game, several of the above, none of the above, of what?

    G. E. L. Owen writes, powerfully and relevantly, in "Aristotle on the Snares of Ontology" in *New Essays on Plato and Aristotle*, ed. Renford Bambrough (London: Routledge & Kegan Paul; New York: Humanities Press, 1965), pp. 69 — 95, "when he [Aristotle] comes to set up his own general metaphysics of 'being' he founds it on the claim that the different senses of 'exist' are systematically connected; and this leads him to deny that 'exist' is really homonymous (*Metaphysics* G: 1003a 33 — b 19). There is a similar reconsideration in his mature ethics when he allows that 'good' is after all not an instance of *chance* homonymy (*Nichomachean Ethics* A 1096b 26 — 7)" [italics in text].

    Let me say (if you'll be charitable) that I believe and think I discern something univocal, really-deep-down-clear, in the range of meaning of *good* (*value*) and in the range of meaning of *true* and *exist*. I think that those concepts may well be in some real sense indefinable because more fundamental than any other concepts or words we could use to define them.

    I believe and discern that these concepts are truly fundamental to our grasp and use of language, our dealing with reality. I further believe and discern that those concepts are not just the inescapable presuppositions of the human mind, which could be — unsayably and unimaginably — other; but that those concepts are veridical because the gifts of God, to Whom, for which, we should be grateful.

5. See Thomas Hobbes, *Leviathan*, in *The English Works of Thomas Hobbes*, ed. William Molesworth, 11 vols., 1839 for vol. 3; Reprint ed. (Aalen, Germany: Scientia Verlag, 1966), 3: 138 — 139, where he defines "COMPLAISANCE" as "*that every man strive to accomodate himself to the rest*," p. 138 (italics in text).

6. For example, Martin Heidegger's assertion "Denn das Fragen ist die Frommigkeit des Denkens" ["For questioning is the piety of thinking"] in "Die Frage nach der Technic" ["The Question of Technology"] in *Vortröge and Aufsätze* [Lectures and Essays], 3rd ed. (Pfullingen, Germany: Gunther Neske, 1967), part 1, p. 36. Cf. the discussion of the phrase in "Translator's Preface," Martin Heidegger, *The Piety of Thinking*, ed. James C. Hart and John C. Maraldo (Bloomington and London: Indiana University Press, 1976), p. [ix]. The assertion at least strongly hints that questioning has become an end (and, as such, a substitute for religious piety). Cf. Heidegger, "Principles of Thinking," *Piety*, ed. Hart, p. 58: "Not until we are sufficiently experienced in our thinking, in the scope of its essential presencing, will we be able to acknowledge another thinking as strange and to listen to it as estranging in its abundant strangeness?" (translating from "Grundsätze des Denkens," *Jahrbuch für Psychologie und Psychotherapie* 6 [1958]: p. 41). Is he seeking, through the estranging, further-knowledge (gainable or not) or is he seeking the seeking of the estranging?

    In his *An Introduction to Metaphysics*, trans. Ralph Manheim (New Haven: Yale University Press, 1959) (For German text, see Martin Heidegger, *Einführung in die Metaphysik* [Tubingen, Germany: Max Niemeyer, 1953]), Heidegger strongly intends to reconstitute philosophy by returning to and truly reconsidering some Greek texts vis-a-vis Being. He writes (pp. 101 — 102; German text, p. 77), "Only now [after the preliminary steps of the book have been taken] are we in a position, on the basis of a more appropriate view of being as the Greeks saw it, to take the decisive step which will open to us the inner relationship, between being and appearance." He seeks that relationship, attempts the decisive step, by exploring passages and concepts of Sophocles (pp. 106 — 108; German text, pp. 82 — 83), Parmenides (esp. pp. 110 — 114; German text, pp. 83 — 87), and Heraclitus (pp. 114 — 116; German text, pp. 87 — 88). Is he getting somewhere? It sounds very much like it.

On the last page of the book (p. 206, italics in text; German text, p. 157) he writes, "The true problem is what we do not know and what, insofar as we know it *authentically*, namely as a problem, we know only *questioningly*.

To know how to question means to know how to wait, even a whole lifetime." And then?

7. Peter Geach, *The Virtues* (Cambridge and New York: Cambridge University Press, 1977), p. 16.
8. Paul Ramsey, "Learning Goodness," in *The Keepers* (New York: Irvington Publishers, 1984), p. 97.

BIBLIOGRAPHY

Anderson, Howard; and John S. Shea. Ed. *Studies in Criticism and Aesthetics, 1660-1800: Essays in Honor of Samuel Holt Monk.* Minneapolis: University of Minnesota Press, 1967. Esp. the essays by Irvin Ehrenpreis, Lillian Feder, Walter J. Hipple, Jr., Earl Miner, and Paul Ramsey. (See as separate entries.)

Anscombe, G. E. M. "On Brute Facts." *Analysis.* 18(1958): 69-72.

Anscombe, G. E. M. "Modern Moral Philosophy." In Hudson, *Is-Ought* [q.v.], pp. 173-195.

Anscombe, G. E. M.; and Peter Geach. *Three Philosophers.* Ithaca: Cornell University Press, 1961.

Anselm of Canterbury. "De Veritate." *Opera Omnia.* 5 vols. Edinburgh: Thomas Nelson, 1940-1951 (1946 for vol. 1.), vol. 1, pp. [169]-199.

Anselm of Canterbury. "On Truth." *Anselm of Canterbury.* 4 vols. Ed. and Trans. Jasper Hoskins and Herbert Richardson. Toronto and New York: Edwin Mellen Press, 1976, vol. 2, pp. 75-102.

Aquinas, Thomas. *Summa Theologica.* Ed. Thomas Gilby. 60 vols. Cambridge: Blackfriars, 1960 for vol. 18. [See also Busa, Roberto. *Index Thomisticus*]

Aristotle. *The Poetics.* Trans. W. Hamilton Fyfe, in Aristotle, *The Poetics*; 'Longinus', *On the Sublime*; Demetrius, *On Style.* The Loeb Classical Library. London: William Heinemann; Cambridge: Harvard University Press, 1965.

Aristotle. *Posterior Analytics.* Trans. Jonathan Barnes. Oxford: Clarendon Press, 1975.

Aristotle. *Prior and Posterior Analytics.* Ed. W. D. Ross. Oxford: Clarendon Press, 1949.

Auden, W. H. *The Dyer's Hand.* New York: Random House, 1962.

Austin, J. L. *How to Do Things with Words.* Oxford: Clarendon Press, 1962.

Austin, J. L. "The Meaning of a Word." In Caton, *Philosophy and* [q.v.], pp. 1-21.

Austin, J. L., P. F. Strawson, and D. P. Cousin. "Truth." [A Symposium]. *Aristotelian Society Proceedings.* 1950. Supplementary Vol. 14, pp. 111-128, 129-156, 157-172 respectively.

Ayer, A. J. *Foundations of Empirical Knowledge.* London: Macmillan; New York: St. Martin's Press, 1955.

Baier, K. See Toulmin and Baier.

Bambrough, Renford. "Aristotle on Justice," In Bambrough, *Plato and Aristotle* [q.v.], pp. 159-174.

Bambrough, Renford. Ed. *New Essays on Plato and Aristotle.* New York: Humanities Press; London: Routledge and Kegan Paul, 1965. Esp. the essays by Renford Bambrough and G. E. L. Owen . (See as separate entries.)

Bambrough, Renford. *Moral Scepticism and Moral Knowledge.* London: Routledge and Kegan Paul, 1970.

Bambrough, Renford. *Reason, Truth, and God.* London: Methuen, 1969.

Barfield, Owen. *The Rediscovery of Meaning and Other Essays*. Middletown, CT: Wesleyan University Press, 1977.

Barthes, Roland. *Critical Essays*. Trans. Richard Howard. Evanston: Northwestern University Press, 1972.

Barthes, Roland. *A Lover's Discourse*. Trans. Richard Howard. New York: Hill & Wang, 1978.

Barthes, Roland. *Mythologies*. Trans. Annette Lavers. New York: Hill & Wang, 1972.

Barthes, Roland. *Le Plaisir du Texte*. Paris: Éditions du Seuil, 1973.

Barthes, Roland. *The Pleasure of the Text*. Trans. Richard Miller. New York: Hill & Wang, 1975.

Belth, Marc. "The Differentiating Curriculum: A Humane Approach." *Humanities in the South*. 49(Spring 1979): [1]-4.

Benedict, Ruth. *Patterns of Culture*. New York: Houghton Mifflin, 1934.

Berkeley, George. *The Principle of Human Knowledge and Three Dialogues between Hylas and Philonous*. Ed. G. J. Warnock. Cleveland and New York: Meridian Books, 1963.

Berlin, Isaiah. *Concepts and Categories*. New York: Viking Press, 1979.

Bernard, Jessie. "The Art of Science." *American Sociological Review*, 55(1959): 1-9.

The Bible, King James Version.

Black, Max. "The Gap between "Is" and "Should"." In Hudson, *Is-Ought* [q.v.], pp. 99-113.

Black, Max. *Models and Metaphors*. Ithaca, New York: Cornell University Press, 1962.

Black, Max. Ed. *Philosophical Analysis*. 1950. Reprint ed., [Freeport, N.Y.]: Books for Libraries Press, 1971. Esp the essays by Herbert Feigl, Margaret MacDonald, and Norman Malcolm. (See as separate entries.)

Blackmur, Richard P. *Language as Gesture*. New York: Harcourt Brace, 1952.

Blackmur, Richard P. *The Lion and the Honeycomb*: New York: Harcourt Brace, 1955.

Blanshard, Brand. *Reason and Goodness*. New York: Macmillan; London: G. Allen and Unwin, 1961.

Bloom, Harold. *The Anxiety of Influence*. New York: Oxford University Press, 1973.

Booth, Wayne C. *Modern Dogma and the Rhetoric of Assent*. Chicago and London: University of Chicago Press, 1974.

Bowers, Fredson. *On Editing Shakespeare*. Charlottesville, VA: University Press of Virginia, 1966.

Bowman, Claude C. "Evaluations and Values Consistent With the Scientific Study of Society." *American Sociological Review*. 8(1943): 306-312.

Boyd, John D. *The Function of Mimesis and Its Decline*. Cambridge: Harvard University Press, 1968.

Brandt, Richard B. Ed. *Value and Obligation*. New York: Harcourt Brace and World, 1961. Esp. the section on Ethical Relativism.

Broad, C. D. *Five Types of Ethical Theory*. London: K. Paul, French, Trubner, 1930.

Broad, C. D. *Kant*. Ed. C. Lewy. New York and Cambridge: Cambridge University Press, 1978.

Brooks, Cleanth; and William K. Wimsatt, Jr. *Literary Criticism: A Short History*. New York: Alfred A. Knopf, 1957.

Bruford, Walter H. "Literary Criticism and Sociology." In Strelka, *Literary Criticism and Sociology* [q.v.], pp. 1-20.

Burke, Kenneth. *The Philosophy of Literary Form*. 3rd ed. Berkeley: University of California Press, 1973.

Busa, Roberto. Comp. *Index Thomisticus*. 56 vols. Stuttgart, West Germany: Frommann/Holzboog, 1974-1976, 1979-1980.

Butler, Joseph. *Butler's Fifteen Sermons Preached at the Rolls Chapel and A Dissertation of the Nature of Virtue*. Ed. with Intro. by T. A. Roberts. London: S.P.C.K., 1970.

Cahn, Edmund. See Ramsey, *Moralists*.

Carnap, Rudolf. *Philosophy and Logical Syntax*. London: K. Paul, French, Trubner, 1935.

Caton, Charles E. Ed. *Philosophy and Ordinary Language*. Urbana: University of Illinois

Press, 1963. Esp. essays by J. L. Austin, and by S. E. Toulmin and K. Baier. (See as separate entries.)

Charles, R. H. *The Decalogue*. Edinburgh: T. and T. Clark, 1923.

Chatman, Seymour. Ed. *Literary Style*. New York and London: Oxford University Press, 1971.

Chatman, Seymour; and Samuel R. Levin. Ed. *Essays on the Language of Literature*. Boston: Houghton Mifflin, 1967.

Cogley, John, and others. *Natural Law and Modern Society*. Center for the Study of Democratic Institutions. Cleveland: World, 1963.

Collingwood, R. G. *An Essay On Metaphysics*. Oxford: Clarendon Press, 1940.

Connor, George. *Hints and Guesses*. Chattanooga: St. Peter's Episcopal Church, 1982. Cincinnati: Forward Movements Publications, forthcoming.

Copleston, Frederick. *Philosophies and Philosophers*. New York: Barnes and Noble, 1976. Esp. "The History of Philosophy: Relativism and Recurrence."

Cousin, D. R. See Austin, J. L. "Truth."

Culler, Jonathan. "Literary Competence." In Freeman, *Modern Stylistics*, pp. 24-41.

Darwin, Charles. *The Descent of Man*. 2nd ed. New York: Hurst, 1874.

Davie, Donald. *Articulate Energy: An Inquiry into the Syntax of English Poetry*. 1st Amer. ed. New York: Harcourt and Brace, 1958.

de Man, Paul. *Allegories of Reading: Figural Language in Rousseau, Nietzsche, Rilke, and Proust*. New Haven: Yale University Press, 1979.

de Man, Paul. *Blindness and Insight: Essays in the Rhetoric of Contemporary Criticism*. 2nd rev. ed. Minneapolis: University of Minnesota Press, 1983.

Derrida, Jacques. *La Dissémination*. Paris: Éditions du Seuil, 1972.

Derrida, Jacques. *Disseminations*. Trans. Barbara Johnson. Chicago: University of Chicago Press, 1981.

Derrida, Jacques. *De La Grammatologie*. Paris: Éditions du Seuil, 1976.

Derrida, Jacques. *Of Grammatology*. Trans. Gayatri Spivak. Baltimore: Johns Hopkins University Press, 1976.

Derrida, Jacques. *Writing and Difference*. Trans. Alan Bass. Chicago: University of Chicago Press, 1978.

Derrida, Jacques. *L'écriture et la différence*. [Paris]: Éditions du Seuil, 1967.

Driver, S. R. *An Introduction to the Literature of the Old Testament*. New ed. New York: Charles Scribner's Sons, 1950.

Dryden, John. *Of Dramatic Poesy and Other Critical Essays*. Ed. George Watson. 2 vols. Everyman's Library. New York: E. P. Dutton; London: J. M. Dent and Sons, 1962.

Durkheim, Emile. *Emile Durkheim on the Division of Labor in Society*. Ed. George Simpson. New York: Macmillan, 1933.

Durkheim, Emile. *De La Division du Travail Social*. 2nd ed. Paris: Félix Alcan, 1902.

Durkheim, Emile. *The Rules of Sociological Method*. Trans. Sarah A. Soloway and John H. Mueller. Ed. George E. G. Catlin. 1st paper ed. New York: Free Press, 1964.

Dworkin, Ronald M. See Summers, *Legal Philosophy*.

Dykes, J. Oswald. *The Law of the Ten Words*. London: Hodder and Stoughton, 1884.

Ehrenpreis, Irvin. "The Cistern and the Fountain." In Anderson, *Criticism and Aesthetics* [q.v.], pp. 156-175, esp. p. 175.

Eliot, T.S. *For Lancelot Andrewes: Essays on Style and Order*. London: Faber & Gwyer, 1928.

Eliot, T.S. *The Sacred Wood*. London: Methuen, 1920.

Ellul, Jacques. *The Theological Foundation of Law*. Trans. Marguerite Weiser. New York: Doubleday, 1948.

Emerson, Ralph Waldo. *Poems*. vol. 9 of *The Complete Works of Ralph Waldo* Emerson (1903-1904). Reprint ed. New York: AMS Press, 1979.

Empson, William. *Seven Types of Ambiguity*. London: Chatto & Windus, 1930.

Feder, Lillian. "Sermo or Satire: Pope's Definition of His Art." In Anderson, *Criticism and Aesthetics* [q.v.], pp. 140-155.

Feigl, Herbert. "De Principiis Non Disputandum . . . [spaced periods in text]. In Black, *Philosophical Analysis* [q.v.], pp. 113-147.

Fish, Stanley, assisted by Ellen S. Mankoff. *Is There a Text in This Class?: Authority of Interpretive Communities.* Cambridge: Harvard University Press, 1980.

Flew, Antony. Ed. *Essays in Conceptual Analysis.* New York: St. Martin's Press; London: Macmillan, 1966. Esp. the essay by Peter Herbst.

Flew, Antony. "On Not Deriving "Ought" from "Is"." In Hudson, *Is-Ought* [q.v.], pp. 135-143.

Fowler, Roger. *The Languages of Literature: Some Linguistic Contributions to Criticism.* London: Routlege & Kegan Paul, 1971.

Frankena, W. K. "The Naturalistic Fallacy." *Mind.* 48(1939): 464-477.

Freeman, Donald C. Ed. *Essays in Modern Stylistics.* London and New York, 1981. Esp. the essays by Jonathan Culler and M. A. K. Halliday. (See as separate entries.)

Frege, Gottlob. *The Basic Laws of Arithmetic.* Ed. and Trans. Montgomery Furth. Berkeley and Los Angeles: University of California Press, 1964.

Frege, Gottlob. *Begriffschrifft: A Formula Language, Modeled upon that of Arithmetic, or Pure Thought.* In *Frege and Godel.* Ed. Jean Von Heigenoort. Cambridge, MA: Harvard University Press, 1970,

Frege, Gottlob. *Begriffschrifft Und Andere Aufsätze.* 1897. Reprint ed., Hildesheim, Germany: Georg Olms, 1964.

Frege, Gottlob. *Grundgesetze der Arithmetik.* 1893. Reprint ed. Hildesheim, Germany: George Olms, 1962.

Frege, Gottlob. *Kleine Schriften.* Ed. Ignacio Angelelli. Hildesheim, Germany: Georg Olms. 1967.

Frege, Gottlob. *Logical Investigations.* Ed. Peter Geach. Trans. Peter Geach and R. H. Stoothoff. New Haven: Yale University Press, 1977.

Frege, Gottlob. *Translations from the Philosophical Writings of Gottlob Frege.* Ed. Peter Geach and Max Black. Oxford: Basil Blackwell, 1970.

Fried, Charles. *Rights and Wrong.* Cambridge, MA; and London: Harvard University Press, 1978.

Fuller, Lon. *The Morality of Law.* New Haven: Yale University Press, 1964.

Furfey, Paul. *The Scope and Method of Sociology: A Metasociological Treatise.* New York: Harper, 1953.

Geach, Peter. "Aquinas." In Anscombe and Geach, *Three Philosophers.* [q.v.], pp. 69-125.

Geach, Peter. *Logic Matters.* Berkeley and Los Angeles: University of California Press, 1972.

Geach, Peter. *The Virtues.* Cambridge and New York: Cambridge University Press, 1977.

Gilby, Thomas. *Phoenix and Turtle.* London and New York: Longmans, Green, 1950.

Ginsberg, Morris. *Essays in Sociology and Social Philosophy.* Vol. 1, *On the Diversity of Morals.* New York: Macmillan, 1957.

Ginsberg, Ralph Bertram. *Anomie and Aspiration.* New York: Arno Press, 1980.

Gleason, Robert W. *Jahweh: The God of the Old Testament.* Englewood Cliffs, NJ: Prentice-Hall, 1964.

Goldman, Solomon. *The Ten Commandments.* Ed. Maurice Samuel. Chicago: University of Chicago Press, 1956.

Gosse, Edmund. *Father and Son.* New ed. London: William Heinemann, 1928.

Gosse, Philip Henry. *Omphalos.* London: John Van Voorst, 1857.

Graff, Gerald. *Literature against Itself.* Chicago: University of Chicago Press, 1979.

Grindel, Carl W. See Ramsey, R. Paul.

Hadzsits, George Depue. *Lucretius and his Influence.* New York: Longmans, Green, 1935.

Halliday, M. A. K. "Linguistic Function and Literary Style." In Freeman, *Modern Stylistics,* pp. 325-360.

Hammurabi. *The Code of Hammurabi of Babylon about 2250 B.C.* Ed. and Trans. Robert

Francis Harper. Transliteration of the Babylonian Text and an English translation. Chicago: University of Chicago Press, 1904.

Hardison, O. B. *The Enduring Monument.* Chapel Hill, NC: University of North Carolina Press, 1962.

Hardison, O. B. Ed. *English Literary Criticism: The Renaissance.* New York: Appleton-Century-Crofts, 1963.

Hare, R. M. "Descriptivism." In Hudson, *Is-Ought* [q.v.], pp. 240-258.

Hare, R. M. *The Language of Morals.* Oxford: Oxford University Press, 1952.

Harman, Gilbert, *The Nature of Morality.* New York: Oxford University Press, 1977. Esp. "Custom and Relation."

Hart, H. L. A. *The Concept of Law.* Oxford: Oxford University Press, 1961.

Hart, Hornell. "Value Judgements in Sociology." *American Sociological Review.* 3(1938): 862-867.

Hartman, Geoffrey H. *Beyond Formalism: Literary Essays 1958-1970.* New Haven: Yale University Press, 1970.

Hastings, James. Ed. *A Dictionary of Christ and the Gospel.* 2 vols. New York: Charles Scribner's Sons, 1906, 1908. Esp. for article on Golden Rule.

Hegel, Georg W. F. *Hegel's Science of Logic.* Trans. W. H. Johnston and L. G. Struthers. 2 vols. New York: MacMillan; London: George Allen and Unwin, 1929.

Hegel, Georg W. F. *Phenomenology of Spirit.* Trans. A. V. Miller. Oxford: Clarendon, 1977.

Hegel, Georg Wilhelm Friedrich. *Wissenschaft der Logik.* Ed. Georg Lasson. 2 vols. 1932. Reprint ed. Hamburg, Germany: Felix, Meiner, 1971.

Heidegger, Martin. *Being and Time.* Trans. John Macquarrie and Edward Robinson. New York: Harper, 1962.

Heidegger, Martin. *Einführung in die Metaphysik.* Tubingen, Germany: Max Niemeyer, 1953.

Heidegger, Martin. "Grundsätze des Denkens." *Jahrbuch fur Psychologie und Psychotherapie.* 6(1958): 33-41.

Heidegger, Martin. *An Introduction to Metaphysics.* Trans. Ralph Manheim. New Haven: Yale University Press, 1957.

Heidegger, Martin. *The Piety of Thinking.* Ed. James C. Hart and John C. Maraldo. Bloomington and London: Indiana University Press, 1976.

Heidegger, Martin. *Vortröge und Aufsätze.* 3rd ed. Pfullingen, Germany: Gunther Neske, 1967.

Herbst, Peter. See Flew, Antony.

Hinman, Charlton. *Printing and Proofreading of the First Folio of Shakespeare.* 2 vols. Oxford: Clarendon Press, 1963.

Hipple, Walter J., Jr. "Philosophical Language and the Theory of Beauty in the Eighteenth Century." In Anderson, *Criticism and Aesthetics,* [q.v.], pp. 213-231.

Hirsch, E. D. *Validity in Interpretation.* New Haven: Yale University Press, 1967.

Hirsch, Samson Raphael. Trans. and Ed. *The Psalms.* vol. 1 (Books 1 & 2). New York: Philipp Feldheim, 1960.

Hobbes, Thomas. *Leviathan,* in vol. 3 of *The English Works of Thomas Hobbes.* Ed. William Molesworth. 11 vols. 1839 for vol. 3. Reprint ed., Aalem, Germany: Scientia Verlag, 1966.

Holmer, Paul. *The Grammar of Faith.* San Francisco: Harper and Row, 1978.

Homer. *The Odyssey.* Trans. Robert Fitzgerald. Garden City, NY : Doubleday, 1963.

Homer. *The Odyssey.* Trans. A. T. Murray. The Loeb Classical Library. Cambridge: Harvard University Press; London: William Heinemann, 1919.

Hudson, William Donald. Ed. *The Is-Ought Question.* New York: St. Martin's Press, 1969. Esp. essays by G. E. M. Anscombe, Max Black, Antony Flew, R. M. Hare, and J. R. Searle. (See as separate entries.)

Hume, David. *Enquiries concerning Human Understanding and concerning the Principles of*

Morals. Ed. L. A. Selby-Bigge. 3rd ed. Text revised and notes by P. H. Nidditch. Oxford: Clarendon Press, 1975.

Hume, David. *The Life of David Hume, Esq. Written by Himself.* London: W. Strahan and T. Cadell, 1777.

Hume, David. *A Treatise of Human Nature.* Ed. L. A. Selby-Bigge. Oxford: Clarendon Press, 1888.

Hynes, Samuel. Ed. *English Literary Criticism: Restoration and 18th Century.* New York: Appleton-Century-Crofts, 1963.

Jacob, B. "The Decalogue." *Jewish Quarterly Review.* New ser. 14(1923): 141-187.

Kant, Immanuel. *Critique of Pure Reason.* Ed. Norman Kemp Smith. New York: Modern Library, 1958.

Kant, Immanuel. *Kritik der Reinen Vernunft.* Ed. Karl Kehrbach. Leipzig, Germany: Philipp Reclam the younger, n.d. [Preface by editor dated 1878.]

Katsoff, Louis O. *Logic and the Nature of Reality.* 2nd ed. The Hague, Netherlands: Martinus Nijhoff, 1967.

Kelsen, Hans. *General Theory of Law and State.* New York: Russell and Russell, 1961.

Kenny, Antony. *The Anatomy of the Soul.* Oxford: Basil Blackwell, 1973.

Kluckhohn, Clyde. "Ethical Relativity: Sic et Non." *Journal of Philosophy.* 52 (1955): 663-677.

Kohler, Wolfgang. *The Place of Value in a World of Fact.* New York: Liveright, 1938.

Krausz, Michael, and Jack W. Meiland. Ed. *Relativism: Cognitive and Moral.* Notre Dame and London: University of Notre Dame Press, 1982.

Krieger, Murray. "The Critic as Person and Persona." In Strelka, *Personality of Critic* [q.v.], pp. 70-92.

Kupperman, Joel. *Philosophy: The Fundamental Problems.* New York: St. Martin's Press, 1978. Esp. "The Nature of Ethics."

La Rue, Gerald. *Old Testament Life and Literature.* Boston: Allyn and Bacon, 1968.

Lepley, Ray. *Verifiability of Value.* New York: Columbia University Press, 1964.

Lewis, Clarence I. *An Analysis of Knowledge and Valuation.* La Salle, IL: Open Court, 1946.

Lewis, C. S. *The Abolition of Man.* Collier Books. New York: Crowell-Collier, 1962.

Little, Elbert L. *The Audubon Society Field Guide to North American Trees: Eastern Region.* New York: Alfred A. Knopf, 1980.

Longinus. *On the Sublime.* In Aristotle, *Poetics,* Longinus, Demetrius [q.v.].

Lucretius. *De Rerum Natura.* Ed. William Ellery Leonard and Stanley Barney Smith. Madison, WI; and London: University of Wisconsin Press, 1968.

Lucretius. *Lucretius on the Nature of Things.* Trans. Cyril Bailey. Oxford: Clarendon Press, 1910.

Lundberg, George A. "Contemporary Positivism in Sociology." *American Sociological Review.* 4(1939): 42-55.

MacDonald, Margaret. "Ethics and the Ceremonial Use of Language." In Black, *Philosophical Analysis* [q.v.], pp. 198-215.

McTaggart, J. McT. Ellis. *Philosophical Studies.* Ed. S. V. Keeling. 1934. Reprint ed. Freeport, NY: Books for Libraries Press, 1966.

MacIntyre, Alasdair. *After Virtue.* Rev. ed. Notre Dame, IN: University of Notre Dame Press, 1983.

Malcolm, Norman. "The Verification Argument." In Black, *Philosophical Analysis* [q.v.], pp. 229-279.

Mannheim, Karl. *Ideology and Utopia: An Introduction to the Sociology of Knowledge.* Trans. Louis Wirth and Edward Shils. New York: Harcourt Brace, 1936.

Mankoff, Ellen S. See Fish, Stanley.

Maritain, Jacques. See Ramsey, *Moralists.*

Maurer, Armand A. *About Beauty: a Thomistic Interpretation.* Houston: Center for Thomistic Studies, University of St. Thomas [in conjunction with or sold by University of Notre Dame Press, Notre Dame, IN], 1983.

Mead, Margaret. "Some Anthropological Considerations Concerning Natural Law." *Natural Law Forum.* 6(1961): 51-64.

Meilaender, Gilbert C. *The Theory and Practice of Virtue.* Notre Dame, IN: University of Notre Dame Press, 1984.

Michaeli, F. "Law: O. T." *A Companion to the Bible.* Gen. ed. J. J. von Allman. New York: Oxford University Press, 1958, pp. 224-227.

Miner, Earl. "Chaucer in Dryden's *Fables.*" In Anderson, *Criticism and Aesthetics* [q.v.], pp. 58-72.

Miner, Earl. *Dryden's Poetry.* Bloomington and London: Indiana University Press, 1967.

Monk, Samuel Holt. See Anderson, Howard.

Monroe, D. H. *Empiricism of Ethics.* Cambridge: Cambridge University Press, 1967. Esp. "Fact and Values" and "The Defence of Relation."

Montgomery, J. A. See Robinson, Henry Wheeler.

Moore, G. E. *Philosophical Papers.* London: George Allen and Unwin; New York: Macmillan, 1959. Esp. the essays "Is Goodness a Quality?" and "Proof of an External World." Also in a Collier Books edition, New York: Crowell-Collier, 1962.

Moore, G. E. *Principia Ethica.* Cambridge: Cambridge University Press, 1903.

Mowinckel, D. Sigmund. *Le Decalogue.* Paris: Libraire Felix Alcan, 1927.

O'Connor, J. D. *Aquinas and Natural Law.* New York: St. Martin's Press, 1968.

Olen, Jeffrey. "Theories, Interpretations, and Aesthetic Qualities." *Journal of Aesthetics and Art Criticism.* 35(1977): 425-431.

Ong, Walter J. *The Presence of the Word: Some Prolegomena for Cultural and Religious History.* New Haven: Yale University Press, 1967.

Owen, G. E. L. "Aristotle on the Snares of Ontology," in Bambrough, *Plato and Aristotle* [q.v.], pp. 69-95.

Parmenides. *Parmenides.* Ed. Leonardo Taran. Princeton: Princeton University Press, 1965.

Pearson, Karl. *The Grammar of Science.*, London: Adam and Charles Black, 1911.

Perry, Thomas D. *Morals Reasoning and Truth: An Essay in Philosophy and Jurisprudence.* Oxford: Clarendon Press, 1976.

Pieper, Josef. *Four Cardinal Virtues.* Notre Dame, IN: University of Notre Dame Press, 1966.

Plato. *Theaeteus and Sophist.* Ed. Harold North Fowler. The Loeb Classical Library. Cambridge: Harvard University Press; London: William Heinemann, 1942.

Polanyi, Michael. *Personal Knowledge.* Chicago: University of Chicago Press, 1958.

Pope, Alexander. *Imitations of Horace.* Ed. John Butt. 2nd ed. of this volume. The Twickenham Edition. New Haven: Yale University Press; London: Methuen, 1953.

Popper, Karl R. *The Logic of Scientific Discovery.* New York: Basic Books, 1959.

Popper, Karl R. *The Open Society and Its Enemies.* 2 vols. 5th ed. Princeton: Princeton University Press, 1966.

Prior, Arthur N. *Logic and the Basis of Ethics.* Oxford: Clarendon Press, 1949.

Quinn, Philip L. *Divine Commands and Moral Requirements.* Oxford: Clarendon Press, 1978.

Quine, W. V. *Word and Object.* Cambridge: Technological Press of the Massachusetts Institute of Technology, 1960.

*Ramsey, Paul. *Basic Christian Ethics.* New York: Scribner, 1950.

*Ramsey, Paul. Ed. *Nine Modern Moralists.* New York and Toronto: New American Library, 1962. Esp. the essay by Jacques Maritain and Edmund Cahn.

*Ramsey, R. Paul. "Christian Ethics and the Future of Humanism." In *God, Man, and Philosophy.* Ed. Carl W. Grindel. New York: Saint John's University, 1971. pp. 82-91.

Ramsey, Paul. "Absolutism and Judgment." In Strelka, *Personality of Critic* [q.v.], pp. 93-110.

Ramsey, Paul. *The Art of John Dryden.* Lexington: University of Kentucky Press, 1969.

*The theologian at Princeton University, not the author of this book.

Ramsey, Paul. *The Fickle Glass*: *A Study of Shakespeare's Sonnets*. New York: AMS Press, 1979.
Ramsey, Paul. *The Keepers*. New York: Irvington, 1984.
Ramsey, Paul. "Literary Criticism and Sociology." In Strelka, *Literary Criticism and Sociology* [q.v.], pp. 21-29.
Ramsey, Paul. *The Lively and the Just*. Tuscaloosa: University of Alabama Press, 1962.
Ramsey, Paul. "Nature in Criticism." Subsection of "Nature" (pp. 551-556). In *Encyclopedia of Poetry and Poetics*. Ed. Alex Preminger. Associate Editors: Frank J. Warnke and O. B. Hardison. Princeton: Princeton University Press, 1965, p. 555.
Ramsey, Paul. "The Watch of Judgment: Relativism and *An Essay on Criticism*. In Anderson, *Criticism and Aesthetics* [q.v.], pp. 128-139.
Richards, I. A. *The Philosophy of Rhetoric*. New York: Oxford University Press, 1936.
Richards, I. A. *Principles of Literary Criticism*. London: Kegan Paul, 1925.
Riffaterre, Michael. *Semiotics of Poetry*. Bloomington: Indiana University Press, 1978.
Robinson, Henry Wheeler. Ed. *Record and Revelation*. Oxford: Clarendon Press, 1938. Esp. the essays by W. A. L. Elmslie, "Ethics," and J. A. Montgomery, "The New Sources of Knowledge."
Robinson, H. Wheeler. *Inspiration and Revelation in the Old Testament*. Oxford: Oxford University Press, 1946.
Rollins, Hyder Edward. See William Shakespeare, *Sonnets*.
Rudnick, Hans H. "Recent British and American Studies concerning Theories of a Sociology of Literature." In Strelka, *Literary Criticism and Sociology* [q.v.], pp. 270-281.
Russell, Bertrand. *Philosophy*. New York: W. W. Norton, 1927.
Russell, Bertrand. *Sceptical Essays*. New York: W. W. Norton, 1928.
Ryan, Alan. *The Philosophy of the Social Sciences*. New York: Pantheon Books, 1970.
Saintsbury, George. *A History of Criticism and Literary Taste in Europe from the Earliest Texts to the Present Day*. 3 vols. London: Blackwood, 1900-1909.
Sandmel, Samuel. *The Hebrew Scriptures*. New York: Alfred A. Knopf, 1963.
Schoenbaum, Samuel. *Shakespeare's Lives*. New York: Oxford University Press, Oxford: Clarendon Press, 1970.
Searle, J. R. "Deriving "Ought" from "Is": Objections and Replies." In Hudson, *Is-Ought* [q.v.], pp. 261-271.
Searle, J. R. "How To Derive "Ought" from "Is"." In Hudson, *Is-Ought* [q.v.], pp. 240-258.
Searle, J. R. *Speech Acts*. Cambridge: Cambridge University Press, 1969.
Sellars, Wilfred. *Philosophical Perspectives*. Springfield, IL: Charles C. Thomas, 1967. Esp. "Physical Realism" and "Science and Ethics."
Shakespeare, William, *The Sonnets*. Ed. Hyder Edward Rollins. Variorum Ed. of Shakespeare. Philadelphia and London: J. P. Lippincott Co., 1944.
Sidgwick, Henry. *Outlines of the History of Ethics*. 4th ed. London: Macmillan, 1896.
Simon, Yves. *The Tradition of Natural Law*. New York: Fordham University Press, 1965.
Smith, John H. Powis. *The Origin and History of Jewish Law*. Chicago: University of Chicago Press, 1931.
Slote, Michael. *Goods and Virtues*. Oxford: Clarendon Press, 1983.
Spitzer, Leo. *Linguistics and Literary History: Essays in Stylistics*. Princeton: Princeton University Press, 1948.
Stevenson, Charles L. *Ethics and Language*. New Haven: Yale University Press, 1944.
Stevenson, Charles L. *Facts and Values*. New Haven: Yale University Press, 1963.
Strauss, Leo. *Natural Right and History*. Chicago: University of Chicago Press, 1953.
Strawson, P. F. See Austin, J. L. "Truth."
Strelka, Joseph. Ed. *Literary Criticism and Sociology*. University Park, PA, and London: Pennsylvania State University Press, 1973. Esp. the essays by Walter H. Bruford, Paul Ramsey, and Hans H. Rudnick. (See as separate entries.)
Strelka, Joseph. Ed. *The Personality of the Critic*. University Park, PA, and London:

Pennsylvania State University Press, 1973. Esp. the essays by Murray Krieger and Paul Ramsey. (See as separate entries.)

Summers, Robert S. Ed. *Essays in Legal Philosophy*. Berkeley and Los Angeles: University of California Press, 1968. Esp. the essay by Ronald M. Dworkin.

Swift, Jonathan. *Gulliver's Travels 1726*. Ed. Herbert Davis. Introduction by Harold Williams. Rev. ed. The Prose Works of Jonathan Swift. Oxford: Basil Blackwell, 1959.

Tate, Allen. *The Forlorn Demon*. Chicago: Henry Regnery Co., 1953.

Tate, Allen. Ed. *The Language of Poetry*. Princeton: Princeton University Press, 1942.

Taylor, A. E. *Does God Exist?* London: Macmillan and Co., 1948.

Taylor, A. E. *Philosophical Studies*. 1934. Reprint ed. Freeport, NY: Books for Libraries Press, 1968. Esp. the essays "Is Goodness a Quality?" and "Knowing and Believing."

Temple, William. *Nature, Man and God*. London: Macmillan, 1934.

Todd, John. Ed. *Relativism*. Belmont, CA: Wadsworth, 1973.

Toulmin, S. E. and K. Baier. "On Describing." In Caton, *Philosophy and* [q.v.], pp. 194-219.

Toulmin, Stephen. *The Philosophy of Science*. London: Hutchinson University Library, 1953.

Toulmin, Stephen, and June Goodfield. *The Discovery Of Time*. New York: Harper and Row, 1965.

Tuve, Rosamond. *Elizabethan and Metaphysical Imagery: Renaissance Poetic and Twentieth-Century Critics*. Chicago: University of Chicago Press, 1947.

Trowbridge, Hoyt. "The Place of the Rules in Dryden's Criticism." *Modern Philology*, 44(1946): 84-96.

Urban, Wilbur. "Axiology." In Dagobert D. Runes. Ed. *Twentieth Century Philosophy*. New York: Philosophical Library, 1943, pp. 51-73.

Urmson, J. O. "On Grading." *Mind*. 59(1950): 145-169.

Veatch, Henry B. *For an Ontology of Morals*. Evanston: Northwestern University Press, 1971.

Vickers, Brian. Ed. *Rhetoric Revalued*. Binghamton, New York: Center for Medieval and Early Renaissance Studies, State University of New York at Binghamton, 1982.

von Wright, G. H. *Norm and Action*. London: Routledge and Kegan Paul, 1963.

Vyvyan, John. *Shakespeare and Platonic Beauty*. New York: Barnes & Noble, 1970.

Waismann, F. *How I See Philosophy*. Ed. R. Harre. New York: St. Martin's Press; London: Macmillan, 1968.

Wardle, W. L. *The History and Religion of Israel*. Oxford: Oxford University Press, 1936.

Warnock, G. J. *The Object of Morality*. London: Methuen 1971. Esp. "Morality and Knowledge."

Warnock, G. J. *English Philosophy Since 1900*. London and New York: Oxford University Press, 1958.

Weaver, Richard. *The Ethics of Rhetoric*. Chicago: Henry Regnery Co., 1953.

Welch, Adam C. *Deuteronomy: The Framework to the Code*. London: Humphrey Milford for Oxford University Press, 1932.

Wellek, René. *Concepts of Criticism*. New Haven: Yale University Press, 1963.

Wellek, René. *A History of Modern Criticism, 1750-1950*. 4 vols. New Haven: Yale University Press, 1955-.

Wellek, René; and Austin Warren. *Theory of Literature* (1949). 3rd. ed. New York: Harcourt Brace, 1963.

Westermarck, Edward. *Ethical Relativity*. London: Routledge and Kegan Paul, 1932.

Westermarck, Edware Alexander. *The Origin and Development of the Moral Ideas*. 2 vols. 1906-1908. Reprint ed. Freeport, NY: Books for Libraries Press, 1971.

Wild, John. *Plato's Modern Enemies and the Theory of Natural Law*. Chicago, University of Chicago Press, 1953.

Wimsatt, William K. *Day of the Leopards: Essays in Defense of Poems*. New Haven: Yale University Press, 1976.

Wimsatt, William K. See Brooks and Wimsatt, *Literary Criticism*.

Winch, P. G. *The Idea of a Social Science*. London: Routledge and Kegan Paul, 1958.

Winters, Yvor. *In Defense of Reason*. London: Routledge & Kegan Paul, 1947.

Wisdom, John. *Paradox and Discovery*. Berkeley and Los Angeles: University of California Press, 1970.

Wittgenstein, Ludwig. *On Certainty*. Ed. G. E. M. Anscombe and G. H. von Wright. Trans. Denis Paul and G. E. M. Anscombe. German and English texts. New York and Evanston, IL: Harper and Row, 1969.

Wittgenstein, Ludwig. *Philosophical Investigations*. Trans. G. E. M. Anscombe. 3rd ed. New York: Macmillan, 1958.

Wittgenstein, Ludwig. *Tractatus-Logico-Philosophicus*. Trans. D. F. Pears and B. F. McGuiness. Introduction by Bertrand Russell. German and English texts. New York: Humanities Press; London: Routledge and Kegan Paul, 1961.

Yeats, William Butler. *A Vision*. Collier Books. New York: Macmillan: 1966.

Yeats, William Butler. *The Collected Poems of W. B. Yeats*. New York: Macmillan, 1951.

Znaniecki, Florjan. *The Method of Sociology*. New York: Farrar and Rinehart, 1934.

Index of Names

135

Index of Topics